100626

Dynamic Discipleship

Kenneth C. Kinghorn

Dynamic Discipleship

FLEMING H. REVELL COMPANY

OLD TAPPAN, NEW JERSEY

Library of Congress Cataloging in Publication Data

Kinghorn, Kenneth C
    Dynamic discipleship.

    1 Christian life—1960–   I. Title.
BV4501.2.K494   248'.4   73–601
ISBN 0–8007–0591–2

Contents

Preface

THIS IS A BOOK for laymen who are Christians and who desire to become more effective Christian disciples.

In writing, I have sought to present a realistic and candid picture of Christian discipleship. I have no vested interests; I defend no particular denominational tradition. Most definitely, I am not interested in camouflaging the problems inherent in following Christ.

At the same time, I am convinced that Christ's way is the only way to complete human fulfillment. So, in this sense, I am biased. I confess that I am prejudiced in favor of Jesus Christ's exclusive claims.

Now that I have declared my bias, I must also explain my approach to writing. My attitude is not, "That's where you should be, now go there." Such an approach savors of a never-mind-what-I-do-just-do-as-I-say mentality. So in this book I try not to preach or indulge in moralisms.

Neither is my attitude, "Hey, you down there: come up here where I am." Such paternalism would imply that I have already arrived, that I am a have speaking to the have-nots. This certainly is not the case.

Rather, my approach in these pages is, "Don't you hear Christ calling? Let's follow him together."

On several occasions, I have heard the following advice:

"Never preach above your personal experience; only preach on the level to which you have already arrived." But I have never felt free to follow such instruction. The reason is simple: Christians are called to witness to Jesus Christ, not to their present level of Christian maturity.

Ministers frequently confess that they have preached themselves under conviction. This is as it should be. Ministers should grow along with their hearers, even as teachers should learn with their pupils.

One other thing about my approach: I have tried not to coerce the reader. I have sought to respect his dignity and autonomy. The Holy Spirit never bullies people; why should I? Rather than pressure the reader, I have presented certain aspects of Christian discipleship in the light of Scripture as I understand it. I have every confidence that truth needs no defense, only a witness.

Most of the suggestions made in this book were not contrived out of any forethought of writing a book on this subject. Rather, the conclusions in these pages represent the results of my personal quest for satisfying answers to questions about the Christian life. This book developed as I considered how I might best communicate to others my excitement about the possibilities of following Jesus Christ.

I sincerely believe that the Holy Spirit is moving in remarkable ways in our contemporary world. Many nominal Christians are determining to explore the implications of their Christian faith. Thousands of formerly indifferent bystanders are entering a new dimension of living via an individual encounter with Jesus Christ. Others are openly taking a second glance at Christ and are on the threshold of personal commitment. For all such persons this book has been written.

Dynamic Discipleship

1
Who Are You, Anyway?

"WHO AM I, and what am I doing here?"

At one time or another, these questions loom before everyone. A deep vacuum remains in the heart of every human being until he discovers who he really is and why he exists on earth. The current lack of a satisfying answer to these questions has erupted into a colossal identity crisis as man frantically explores many routes in order to find a meaning to life. Pleasure, sex, thirst for power, endless travel, and ceaseless activity are but a few of these routes. Despite the importance of the question, "Who am I?," few persons have found a meaningful answer. Even though we witness a vast explosion of knowledge, many people still fail to understand the mystery of human existence. To use the language of a first-century apostle: "[People] are always learning and yet never able to grasp the truth" (2 Timothy 3:7 PHILLIPS).

But truth is not that far away. God has never been silent. Although man has been slow to listen, God continues to speak. For thousands of years he has revealed truth to the human family—truth about man and truth about God.

In a climactic act of love, God came among us in the person of Jesus Christ. Since that time, man no longer needs to grope along without any answers to life's ultimate questions —the questions about who he is and about why he is here.

Jesus came to do more than tell us about God; he came to show us God. He announced, "I and the Father are one. . . . the Father is in me and I am in the Father" (John 10:30,38).

No attempt is made in these pages to prove that what Jesus said about himself is true. To the Christian believer, Christ's statements are not debatable; they constitute final truth. For the Christian, Jesus stands as the norm of all truth, and what he said shapes all decisions and actions.

Jesus calls all men to himself. "Follow me," is one of the central themes of his ministry. The presupposition behind this book is that Christian discipleship is the highest calling and the grandest destiny of every human being. No greater opportunity exists for mankind.

If one can answer the question, "Who are you, anyway?" by saying, "I am Christ's disciple," he is on his way to complete fulfillment as a person. Let's consider the implications of what it means to be a Christian disciple.

I started thinking seriously about Christian discipleship for the first time when, as a young man just out of college, I came to know Jesus Christ personally. When Christ became the center of my existence, a literal revolution began in my personality. This revolution has been the most exciting thing I have ever experienced, and its effects continue in my life.

As a new convert reading the Bible, I was startled to discover that in the New Testament the word *disciple* is not used exclusively for the twelve original followers of Jesus. The word appears about 260 times in the gospels and in Acts, and it is used most often to include Christians other than the original twelve disciples. In the Book of Acts, *disciple* is the term used most often to refer to Christians. In fact, believers were called disciples *before* they were called Christians.

". . . in Antioch the disciples were for the first time called Christians" (Acts 11:26). Luke, the writer of Acts, uses the word *saint* only four times, and the word *Christian* but twice. But he uses the word *disciple* twenty-two times.

A fair conclusion unfolds: *Every Christian is a disciple.* So the answer to the question, "Who are you, anyway?" is, "If you are a Christian, you are a disciple of Jesus Christ." Some Christians are better disciples than others, but all Christians are disciples. My personal realization that I, too, was a disciple changed my life. I began to want to know more about how I might be a better follower of Jesus Christ.

Up to the time of my conversion to Jesus Christ, my formal schooling had been secular. I had had very little understanding of who Christ was. I knew that he was somehow special, but I did not know much more than that.

I had a professor in college who said, "We are all like Christ, and he is like us. He's just higher on the scale, that's all." Then he went on to explain, "Just say *man* in a loud voice and you have said Christ; say *Christ* in a soft voice and you have man." I have since learned that Jesus Christ is not just superior to other personalities, nor is he merely the best man who has lived. He is in a class by himself. He is divine and "altogether other." In every way he is unique.

Christ's call to discipleship is also unique. Christian discipleship is unlike any other type of relationship. To be sure, there are similarities between Christianity and non-Christian systems. However, the foundation and roots of the Christian way are completely different, not comparable to any other way.

What then is so special about Christian discipleship? Why is it so different from other types of discipleship?

First, *Christian discipleship is unique because it begins with Christ's call to man.* This is another way of saying, "Christianity begins with God, not man." To begin with man's ideas about God is to end with what man can produce or devise. When persons exclude God from their thinking, they invariably arrive at naive optimism or hopeless pessimism. To start with Christ, however, is to end with truth and fulfillment. Our encounter with God starts with his call to us, not with our decision to seek him.

During Jesus' time, in both the Jewish tradition and the Greek philosophical schools, the disciple took the initiative as to which teacher he wanted to follow. Outside Christianity, the same pattern follows even today. We choose the books we want to read, the movies we want to see, the games we want to play. We choose our schools, our professions, and our teachers. We suppose that the same freedom exists in the realm of religion. We assume that we can choose which "God" to follow. But such an assumption is at best only a half-truth.

Jesus said: "You did not choose me, but I chose you . . ." (John 15:16). Every encounter between God and man is initiated by God. He calls us to himself through Jesus Christ. Christ sets in motion all truly valid religious experience.

And Christ calls the most unlikely of us: the sinners, the unworthy, those of us with few talents. Of course the response to his call is up to us; nevertheless, the call first comes from Christ.

Someone may say, "Are you telling me that some are called and some are not called?" Of course not! Christ calls *all* men to follow him and to be his disciples (although not everyone hears and responds). The gospel is universal in scope: it has no distinction of race, class, sex, or status. Christ has no favorites; he beckons every person to be his disciple.

We like to think that we can perform praiseworthy acts for God. But part of the very core of the gospel is precisely that we are unable to merit God's favor. He came to us in Jesus Christ, seeking us out in our lostness. Our ultimate fulfillment as human beings comes only through a personal response to this gracious call. Discipleship begins as we respond to Christ's coming to us.

Second, *Christian discipleship is unique because it is intensely personal.* Every person is converted to Jesus Christ individually—completely alone. There may be others who find Christ at the same time, but each conversion is a private affair. If one is not personally converted, he is not truly converted in a biblical sense.

In Christian discipleship the *person* of Jesus Christ is central. Not knowledge, not religious truth, but Christ himself. Christian discipleship is not the result of embracing an idea; it is a commitment to the person of Jesus Christ. Various philosophical schools coax us to this truth or that idea, to this system or that way of looking at things. Christ doesn't call us to religion; he calls us to himself.

As I struggled to find a meaningful faith in God, for several years I did not find any satisfaction. This was because I failed to apprehend the personal dimension of faith. I was looking for an idea or a solution with which to agree. I did not understand that the real issue is Jesus Christ. In short, I viewed religion as a theory to be accepted and a certain standard of ethical performance to be maintained. My whole understanding revolved around myself and impersonal ideas about religion. What I needed was not precepts about Christ: I just needed Christ himself. Only when I began to apprehend the necessity of a *personal* relationship with Christ did I get on the right track. I had viewed religion from a distance—I was not willing to open myself to the scrutiny of Christ. I preferred to keep my distance from Christ and hide behind some general ideas about religion and morality. That way I could be religious and yet run no risks of real involvement with Christ at a deeply personal level.

But it is not Christ's teaching which empowers the Christian disciple; it is Christ's personal presence. Paul the apostle never urges his readers primarily to submit to Christianity or to Christ's doctrines. Rather he insists on a personal surrender of the self to Christ.

Christian discipleship is basically interpersonal.

Third, *Christian discipleship is unique because it requires a radical obedience.* Christ sets the agenda and he makes the rules. He provides the contract and he gives the stipulations. Christian discipleship is not a business arrangement between two equals. It is a master-disciple relationship. Christ is the Lord; we are his subjects.

We never come to God on our own terms. If we come at all, we must come on his conditions.

I was in a rap session with a group of students in a college in the Midwest when a handsome sophomore said, "I've been thinking about turning to Christ, but there are certain conditions he must meet before I do."

As we talked together, I tried to point out that the only proper attitude we can assume toward Christ is one of surrender. "We can't bargain with God," I said. "The only thing we can do is come to Christ without any demands of our own." This means that we can't insist that God show us a road map of the entire future. We have to trust him to lead us in his own time and in his own way.

One minister said, "When I was a young man in college, I was willing to surrender to God's will if he would only show me what it was. I wanted God to fill in the check for me to see, and then I would gladly sign it. Then I realized that I was asking God to tell me all about the future *before* I trusted him. Finally, I surrendered to God, not knowing fully what he wanted me to do in the years ahead. That day I really met God for the first time."

One of the words Paul often uses to describe himself is *servant* (literally, *bondslave*). Christ is *Lord* and his disciples are *servants*. Christ leads; we follow. He states the rules; we submit.

This does not mean, of course, that we cannot talk to God in prayer about our doubts and hang-ups, for we can. It does mean, however, that the Christian disciple is subject to Christ in all things—things understood and things not yet understood. Knowing God begins with unhesitating surrender to Christ as Lord.

Fourth, *Christian discipleship is unique because it is a way of life.* During the time when Jesus walked among men, the non-Christian world understood discipleship to be a step toward a greater goal. The disciple outgrew his teacher and then went on to bigger achievements. But Christian discipleship is an end in itself!

The greatest event in a person's life occurs when he becomes a disciple of Jesus Christ. This is because Christ offers himself as the only source of authentic living. He said of himself, "I am the Alpha and the Omega, the first and the last, the beginning and the end" (Revelation 22:13). He *is* spiritual reality.

When I was a young man of twenty-two, I was religious—that is, I went to church and supported the church with time and money. I was reasonably upright in character. But I did not enjoy a personal relationship with Christ. I knew *about* Christ, but I did not know him firsthand. I found a vital relationship with Christ only when I temporarily forgot the moralistic advice of well-meaning friends and came to know Jesus Christ personally.

For several months before my conversion to Christ, I experienced an intense spiritual hunger. I did not really know God, and I sensed my need. I talked with more than one minister and I read widely, but spiritual satisfaction eluded me. One day my landlady said to me, "Kenneth, why don't you try reading the Bible?"

"That's a good idea," I responded. "I don't know why I didn't think of that before."

As I read Scripture, I saw that I was going about the matter of being a Christian all wrong. I was looking at the religious life as *something* rather than *Someone*. I had been spending long hours discussing truth (in the abstract, I'm afraid). What I needed was not to know ideas about God. I needed to know God himself.

I found in the Bible that to know Christ is to know God. I discovered such verses as the following: ". . . if you knew me, you would know my Father also" (John 8:19). Then I remembered a verse which I had learned long ago in summer vacation Bible school: "Jesus said to him, 'I am the way, and the truth, and the life; no one comes to the Father, but by me' " (John 14:6). Such verses as these were beginning to change my life. I was getting closer to God than I had ever been.

A few days after reading these verses, I was sitting toward the rear of a large auditorium watching a play. The play was not very good, and my thoughts wandered. As I sat there, I began to talk quietly to God. As I prayed, I surrendered myself to Christ. At that moment I entered the Kingdom! There was no doubt. I had met God. Rather, I should say, "God met me." The conscious presence of Christ filled my life just as surely as air fills our lungs when we inhale.

I did not hear any voice—see flashing lights—or cry—or laugh. I was just conscious that Christ was real and that he had entered my life. I felt as though I had been born all over again. Later, I read Jesus' words, "I say to you, unless one is born anew, he cannot see the kingdom of God" (John 3:3). And I knew by experience what Jesus had been talking about.

Soon, I found some new friends who helped me to grow spiritually in my newfound faith in Christ. I learned to pray. (My prayers up to that time had mostly consisted of the Lord's prayer and "God is great, God is good, let us thank him for our food.") My new friends showed me how important it was to include fellowship with other Christians in my weekly schedule. I am grateful for the strength I gained from my friends in those early months of my walk with Christ. But the advice I received was not an unmixed blessing.

Some of my new friends exhibited inward joy and a real love toward other persons. Others, however, lacked joy; they viewed Christian discipleship as a duty. They gave me the impression that it was a sin to enjoy life or to laugh very much. They tended to criticize others who were not as spiritual as they were.

I wanted none of what the second group had to offer. Indirectly, however, they taught me an important lesson. I saw that Christian discipleship involved serving Christ, not Christ's cause. I also saw that being a Christian does not consist of being a member of an exclusive clique which gives a holier-than-thou impression to others. Causes and cliques cannot sustain one's loyalty and enthusiasm indefinitely. But Christ can! An idea is impersonal; Christ is intensely personal. Christ makes Christian discipleship come alive.

So I learned that Christian discipleship is a daily person-to-person relationship to Jesus Christ. It is a way of life. And what an exciting way I found it to be!

Christian discipleship is quite different from any system of self-improvement. The Christian disciple has access to the resources of the Holy Spirit. In fact, Jesus sends the Holy Spirit to dwell within the heart of every Christian. The Holy Spirit makes Christ increasingly real to the Christian, and through the Spirit Jesus walks with his disciples in every circumstance of life.

Success for a Christian disciple does not depend upon outward circumstances. Fulfillment comes from a source altogether different from such things as money, power, popularity or physical comfort. The Christian is rooted in the eternal Christ, not in temporal circumstances.

I do not say that Christians never feel disappointment. Nor are they spared from such things as disease and financial problems. But Christians have an inner resource—the personal presence of Christ. And Christ can make one adequate for whatever life brings. With Christ one can face life in a new way because he no longer meets obstacles alone.

Does it cost anything to become a disciple of Christ? Yes. It costs you everything you have. The glory of Christian discipleship is that in losing your life for Christ, you find your life. Those who hoard their lives and live selfishly do so at the cost of forfeiting a relationship with Christ. In the end they lose the very things they tried to preserve. Life turns sour and true fulfillment evaporates like a mirage. True life can be found only as one surrenders his life to God and allows God to begin the process of remaking him into a maturing Christian disciple.

A piece of original art work hangs in our den. It is a very simple plaque, covered with brown burlap. On one part of the plaque are two fish carved of black walnut, and five loaves of bread fashioned out of copper. On the other part of the plaque these words stand out: "All I have." Of course, the reference is to the story of the young lad who gave all he had to Jesus—just five loaves and two fish. He did not have very much, and what he did have seemed meager in the face of five thousand hungry persons. But he gave what he had; that was all he could do. Jesus multiplied it: the boy was fed and so were five thousand others.

Christ will multiply and use all that you give to him. Although we are not responsible for the number or quality of talents we have, we are responsible for the way we use them. As we surrender all we have to Christ, he will make us his disciples and use our talents to bless many other persons. Surrender to Jesus Christ does not result in the loss of one's personal freedom or integrity. Rather, it is the beginning of true freedom and the reorientation of one's natural powers around Christ.

Christian discipleship will not rob one of joy or fulfillment. Quite the contrary. Ultimate fulfillment comes *only* to the Christian disciple. Christian disciples have heard Christ's call to new life, and they follow him confidently in willing obedience. They rejoice in their privilege to follow him because they have discovered firsthand that Christ's call to discipleship is an invitation to participate in life at the very highest level.

2

Haze on the Diamond

ONE EVENING in a rural church, a farmer named Karl blurted out, "Christ has might' near ruined me!" His friends had been witnessing to all the good things God had done in their lives. God had cured one man's illness, caused another man's business to prosper, brought an estranged couple back together.

Karl's affairs had not gone smoothly after his conversion to Christ. It seemed to him that, since becoming a Christian six months prior, he had experienced the worst luck in his life. The farm was not doing well—his ulcers had gotten worse— his wife nagged as she always did. Karl grew more and more restless as several other Christians were telling how well things were going for them. And finally, Karl exploded: "Christ has might' near ruined me!"

It is not hard to serve God when everything is going well. It does not take much consecration to keep steady when things work out to our liking. But how are we to react when prayers do not appear to be answered—when God fails to heal a sick loved one—when there does not seem to be any happy ending to a complicated puzzle? What are we to say when the diamond of our Christian experience seems to develop a haze on it? Is God dead, or perhaps on a long vacation, if discipleship is not what we thought it was going to be?

I do not know if you have asked these questions, but I have. I found that after becoming a disciple of Christ, I continued to have problems and unanswered questions. I was bewildered, because somehow I had gotten the idea that Christians did not have any serious problems. I knew that I had plenty of problems: some I had always had, and some I had picked up after becoming a Christian.

Not that God had failed to meet my most basic needs—he had done so! I experienced forgiveness, joy, and a profound sense of spiritual well-being. I belonged to Christ and Christ belonged to me. I had one foot in heaven; but I was aware that I also had one foot very firmly planted in this world with all of its difficulties and problems.

Everyone has obstacles in life; the real issue is how he handles them. I found myself sometimes threatened with anxiety about the future and discouragement about the present. I take no credit for it, but guilt was not a real problem for me after I became a Christian. A sense of Christ's forgiveness was very vivid in my life. He had forgiven me and I knew it. Nevertheless, the threat of worry and discouragement became very real to me.

I have since found that these two temptations are quite common among Christians. They are perhaps the greatest hindrances to effective discipleship. When anxiety and discouragement appear in the life of a Christian, they are really symptoms of a basic lack of trust in God. I like to think of anxiety and discouragement in much the same way as we think of physical symptoms.

For example: The normal temperature of a healthy body hovers around 98.6 degrees Fahrenheit. Body temperature is a good gauge of our state of physical health. Either too high a temperature or too low a temperature indicates a physical problem. An irregular reading of the thermometer tells us that nature is sending up a flare to warn that something is not as it should be.

Spiritual symptoms also appear in our lives. These symptoms can become warnings to us if we listen to them. They indicate a sagging spiritual vitality. Anxiety can be compared to a fever; discouragement can be compared to a chill. To fret is to fall into one ditch, and to surrender to discouragement is to fall into another. I found that sometimes I ran too hot —I worried; sometimes I ran too cold—I became discouraged.

Most Christians experience similar times when they are threatened by emotions which dog them and make life miserable. Sometimes they fume with anxiety and at other times they feel almost overcome with despondency.

Take, as an illustration, the stalwart Martin Luther. He was strong; he was courageous; he was a model of spiritual strength. Yet he had times of terrible anxiety; at other times he had periods of depression. About six years after his famous "Here I Stand" speech before the Diet of Worms, he wrote, "For more than a week I was close to the gates of death and hell. I trembled in all my members. Christ was wholly lost. I was shaken by desperation and blasphemy of God."

I have never been quite that shaken, but I think I know something of how Luther felt. At times, such states of mind as fretting or becoming discouraged have a way of creeping up on us. We do not have to make any conscious decision to begin to worry or to feel sorry for ourselves. These attitudes appear without any invitation. Like the smog, these moods just come. Some Christians have become chronic fretters, while still others are overcome by a what's-the-use-anyhow attitude.

Sometimes we are able to keep our emotions from showing. We are experts at erecting facades. We can hide our defeat under a brave smile with which we try to fool others. But we cannot hide our real feelings from ourselves or from those who really know us well.

It is, of course, very easy to fall prey to those attitudes which will undermine our Christian discipleship. We can fall from victor to victim. In our frenetic world we are bombarded by an array of claims upon our time, our attention and our energy. Our five senses of taste, sight, touch, smell, and hearing are almost constantly besieged by something wanting our attention.

A middle-aged businessman recognized this problem when he said, "I'm so caught up in the daily rat race that I hardly have time to think. I don't have any time to cultivate my relationship with God. And as a result I'm a prime target for anxiety. I don't know what real peace is. Sometimes I think that worry is my middle name."

Circumstances cause many persons deliberately to teach their children to fear. A lady from a large coastal city was in our home recently and in the course of the conversation she said, "We are forced to teach our children to be afraid. For their own good, we teach them to be afraid of the dark, afraid of strangers, afraid to leave anything unlocked. It's a way of life for millions of us."

The effect of much of our contemporary music is anything but soothing. We watch many TV programs which are expressly designed to produce tension. Violence and gloomy pessimism are given wide coverage by our news media. The end result of all this bombardment is that worry and a sense of futility are very much a part of our age.

It is no exaggeration to say that no other period of human history has been characterized by such a frenetic and at times almost insane pace of life. Fear and anxiety are states of *dis-ease* which are hallmarks of the times.

The maturing Christian disciple, however, reminds himself that worry and a sense of futility lurk as destructive intruders. They do not represent God's design for the human family. These emotional states result from our failure to live in harmony with God's plan. Our minds and bodies are not designed to carry the weight of such negative attitudes. We harbor anxiety and discouragement at the expense of our own emotional and physical well-being.

All negative attitudes are simply the result of an improper use of the basic emotions which God has given to us. For example, worry is really the misuse of a natural and very good capacity. God has given to each human being the capacity to relate to the future. Animals have this ability only to a slight degree. And even in this, instinct is responsible for most animal activity. Man, however, to an almost infinite degree, can project into the future. God planned it this way because man is destined for an endless existence. As a wise sage said many centuries ago, "God . . . has put eternity into man's mind . . ." (Ecclesiastes 3:10,11).

Thus, part of man's uniqueness is his ability to plan for, and relate to, the future—a future which extends beyond time into the infinitude of forever. This is one of the many ways man differs from the animals. We are all created in God's image, and part of that image is self-awareness.

But like every other capacity that man has, his awareness

of the future can get out of control. It can become distorted, twisted, perverted, and produce a spiritual drag on his life. A proper concern for the future can degenerate into an unhealthy concern when it becomes separated from God. Anxiety, fretting and worry come from a misdirected concern for the future.

"Anxiety in a man's heart weighs him down . . ." (Proverbs 12:25). This is the conclusion regarding tension written by Solomon many centuries ago. By fretting we obviously can do nothing to change the thing about which we fret. There is no plus to be gained by worry. In fact, worry is less than a zero. It is a minus. Enormous amounts of creative energy and constructive thinking are canceled by the negative act of fretting.

Because some of Paul's converts were ensnared by worry, he wrote to them in a letter, "Have no anxiety about anything, but in everything by prayer and supplication with thanksgiving let your requests be made known to God" (Philippians 4:6).

Jesus expressed his attitude toward worry when he was a guest in the home of Mary, Martha, and Lazarus. Martha made an enormous fuss over Jesus by spending a great deal of time in the kitchen preparing an elaborate meal. As she worked, she became resentful of her sister, Mary, for not helping more and talking less. Jesus spoke kindly but incisively to her in words which are a continual reminder to all of us today: "Martha, Martha, you are anxious and troubled about many things" (Luke 10:41). Elsewhere Jesus said, ". . . do not be anxious about your life . . ." (Matthew 6:25).

If the Bible urges upon us the fear of the Lord, how can this

command be reconciled with the many other biblical pas-
sages telling us to refrain from fear?

The biblical references to the *fear* of the Lord may be
translated *reverence* or *respect* for God. Respect and reverence are wholesome types of fear. Job's ancient speech contained excellent advice when he declared, " 'Behold, the fear
of the Lord, that is wisdom; and to depart from evil is understanding' " (Job 28:28). The Psalmist advised, "the fear of the
LORD is clean, enduring for ever" (Psalms 19:9).

The writers were saying something like this: "God is holy
and his people are not; the beginning of wisdom therefore is
to fear God and to give him proper respect."

Isaiah, the very eloquent prophet, rebuked the Hebrews
for fearing the wrong things—things which other people
feared. He thundered, ". . . do not fear what they fear, nor
be in dread. But the LORD of hosts, him you shall regard as
holy; let him be your fear, and let him be your dread" (Isaiah
8:12,13).

Discussing the dilemma of those who have turned away
from God, Paul observed, " 'There is no fear of God before
their eyes' " (Romans 3:18). Thus, there is a proper fear—the
fear of the Lord. But notice: we are distinctly bidden not to
fear life.

Perhaps many of us fear the wrong things. We are afraid
of life, but we fail to fear (reverence) the Lord. The Bible
emphasizes that the beginning of wisdom is to fear God and
then meet life unafraid.

For several months after I became a disciple of Jesus
Christ, I enjoyed almost perfect peace. I was excited about
my new relationship with God; I experienced an exception-

ally deep sense of contentment. Things went well for me, and I assumed that this almost uninterrupted joy would continue indefinitely. But gradually I began to experience a drag on my spiritual momentum.

For one thing, I was involved in too many activities. I did not take enough time for sleep, and I failed to eat properly. As a result, I grew physically tired. I did not take into consideration the complex relationship which exists between our physical bodies and our spirits. Perhaps none of us fully understands the meaning of Jesus' statement to Peter, "The spirit indeed is willing, but the flesh is weak" (Matthew 26:41). I was neglecting my body, not being aware that our physical condition has a bearing on our spiritual well-being. My overwork was beginning to affect my spiritual life.

There was something else which caused me to begin to cool off spiritually. My superior at work came to me one day and said something like this: "Kinghorn, what's this I hear about you becoming a religious fanatic? I don't mind if you want to be a Christian; I'm one too," he said, pointing to a ring on his finger which bore the image of a cross. "From now on you had better keep your Christianity confined to church."

This hurt deeply. I have always wanted to be liked—to be accepted. And this mild bit of persecution wounded my ego. After all, I did not want to give a bad impression to anyone.

Smarting under this comment, I remembered a lady I knew who "got converted." She promptly left our church and started a new congregation of her own. She regarded her new congregation as more spiritual than other Christian congregations. Saturday evenings she would play the accordion and preach on the busy sidewalk of the main street in our town. Whenever I saw her preaching in this fashion, I was horrified—terribly embarrassed. I wanted no part of anything like that! So when my superior at work threw cold water on me, I became discouraged. I wondered if, like the lady who left our church, I was giving a holier-than-thou impression. None of us likes to be thought of as odd or peculiar, especially in religion.

Then there was another reason I began to feel sorry for myself. Several of my friends with whom I shared my newfound faith were not the slightest bit impressed. I sensed that some of them would rather I did not come around if I were going to mention Jesus Christ. My sensitive radar picked up such things as a raised eyebrow here and a knowing wink there.

I was discouraged because I was not able to bring all my friends to Christ. I had found in Christ what I had always wanted, but I was not doing a very good job of convincing anyone else.

As I began to think about my situation and to pray about it, I reached two conclusions: First, I was relying on my own strength to be a disciple of Christ; Second, I had not learned how to rely fully upon the Holy Spirit for power and daily inner renewal.

Actually, these two ideas are so closely connected that they come to the same thing: The successful Christian life comes when we realize how little spiritual power we have and how much spiritual power is available in Jesus Christ.

A basic fact which all Christian disciples must learn is that no one can possibly live the Christian life in his own strength. To come to this admission is not easy because it is hard on our egos to confess that we need God's help. At least this was a difficult lesson for me to learn. I prided myself on my ability to do almost anything I set myself to do. But I soon found that I was completely unable to live a consistent Christian life unless God took me in hand and worked a miracle in my life.

Most of us are conditioned to think that everything depends on what we are able to do. This attitude was behind the question of a young man who came to Jesus and asked, "What must we do, to be doing the works of God?"

Jesus replied, "This is the work of God, that you believe in him whom he has sent" (John 6:28, 29).

What Jesus seems to be saying is, "The most important thing that you can *do* is to *believe*. Faith is the greatest work you can perform. *Believing* comes first; then activity follows. But to put *doing* before believing is to miss the most important concept of Christian discipleship." The Christian's activity flows out of his faith.

The fundamental reason Christ sent the Holy Spirit to the church is precisely because Christians lack the power to live adequately.

A false formula:

> Christian conversion + our ability = effective
> discipleship.

A correct formula:

> Christian conversion + Christ's power = effective
> discipleship.

I was making the mistake of thinking that discipleship consisted of how much I did for Christ and how hard I worked at being a Christian. But Christian discipleship does not consist of making our own plans and then executing them in our own energy. Rather, the Christian life consists of obedience and self-surrender.

As in other areas of life, we learn about discipleship by experience. Relying on our own efforts invariably leads us into failure as Christ's disciples. This failure, in turn, produces tension and discouragement. We learn by the experience of failure that we cannot be effective disciples in our own strength—then we can begin to be taught by Christ and to receive his power.

The haze on the diamond will disappear only when we learn to abandon self-effort and start receiving from Christ the power to be Christians.

The life of Christian discipleship properly understood and properly lived will bring a sparkle into life. The Christian need not fall victim to anxiety and discouragement. Through the indwelling Christ he can rise above these negative feelings and become a liberated human being who meets each new challenge with confidence and boundless enthusiasm.

3

Excess Baggage

THE WORK OF THE HOLY SPIRIT was one of the last subjects Jesus discussed with his disciples before he was crucified. In his remarks, Jesus said that the Holy Spirit will ". . . guide you into all the truth" (John 16:13). Certainly, this is a promise that the Holy Spirit will lead us into the truth about God. But more seems implied. The verse says, "*all* the truth." This means also that the work of the Holy Spirit includes leading us into the truth about *ourselves.*

Everyone recognizes that it is quite difficult to understand the complexities of man. Bildad the Shuhite, an ancient friend of Job, was quite right in observing, ". . . for we are but of yesterday, and know nothing, for our days on earth are a shadow" (Job 8:9). What he appears to be saying is that man has a very limited perspective which restricts his knowledge to only a small part of reality.

Even though contemporary man has made amazing discoveries and developed incredible inventions, his knowledge about himself is comparatively minute. Perhaps we know less about man than about any other area of knowledge. Yet, we have the promise of Jesus that the Holy Spirit will lead us into all the truth—including truth about ourselves.

As a new Christian, I was sometimes shocked at the un-Christian behavior of which I was capable. I wondered why

I sometimes acted as I did. Then I remembered having learned somewhere that the human personality can be compared to an iceberg. That is, only a portion of man's mental makeup is on the conscious level. A sizeable part of the mind consists of what some call the *unconscious mind* or the *deep mind*.

Everything we have ever learned or experienced is stored in our unconscious minds. Everything. This is why Paul urged so strongly that we guard with care what we put into our minds. ". . . all that is true, all that is noble, all that is just and pure, all that is lovable and gracious, whatever is excellent and admirable—fill all your thoughts with these things" (Philippians 4:8 NEB).

The unconscious part of us is by no means our enemy. God made us just the way we are—including our unconscious minds. The unconscious mind is God's gift to us, and it can do wonderful things for us. For example, it aids us in creativity, often solving problems for us. However, there may be things present in the deep mind that are not good and that may hinder our spiritual development. Such hurtful deposits constitute part of the Christian's excess baggage.

Each one of us has an array of psychological needs. For example, we need to feel wanted and accepted; we need to find fulfillment in our work and play; we need a sense of security; we need to have a clean conscience.

The Bible does not suggest in any way that these needs are improper or wrong. They are perfectly normal. Psychological needs constitute a natural part of our emotional lives; it is as natural to have emotional needs as it is to have physical needs. As infants and small children we rely almost totally upon others to meet our psychological as well as our physical needs.

Because we live in a sinful and imperfect world, our emotional needs are never perfectly met. And when our emotional and psychological needs are not met, we suffer a degree of maladjustment. I once had a seminary professor who insisted, "We are all a bit neurotic; the only difference is in the degree of our neuroticism." He was right. While some persons have suffered a great deal more emotional maladjustment than others, we all have a less-than-perfect emotional adjustment. These personality maladjustments work against us in our Christian life and create a definite hindrance to effective Christian discipleship. For this reason, we need to define the areas in which they occur and seek to overcome them.

These personality maladjustments may arise from three areas: (1) family life, (2) social life, and (3) personal life.

Some parents have difficulty in communicating love and acceptance to their children. This is an unfortunate shortcoming because a child's self-image is almost totally dependent upon the attitudes communicated to him by his parents.

As an illustration, suppose that two parents are overdemanding of their child and communicate to him the impression that he can never measure up to their almost impossible standards. The parents criticize their child so often that the child thinks to himself: "I'm not worth very much. I'm really not very good because my parents don't like me too well." Such a child will doubtless grow to adulthood with a feeling of inferiority because he concludes—probably unconsciously —that he is inferior to others. He carries his inferiority feelings into his adult life. Later, he may find difficulty in accepting God's forgiving love. If he becomes a Christian, he may live much of his Christian life under a cloud of doubt because he feels unworthy of God.

I know a young wife named Lucille who is the mother of two children. Lucille had an extremely difficult time in her Christian life because of some deep-seated resentments toward her parents. For years, she refused to admit that these feelings existed, pushing them deeper and deeper into her unconscious mind.

She had grown up with several brothers and sisters, but she was the one her mother always bragged about for being "mother's good little girl." Her brothers and sisters made noise and got dirty, as all normal children do. Inwardly, she wanted to join in the fun, but she restrained herself because she was "mother's good little girl."

At the time, of course, Lucille knew nothing of repression nor of pushing resentments deep into the unconscious. But this is what she was doing. Only after she became an adult with children of her own did her resentments rise to the surface, appearing in the form of severe depression.

Some well-meaning friends advised Lucille that she lacked the proper dedication to God. But lack of consecration was not her problem at all. She just needed to allow God to heal the frustrations and the bitterness toward her mother which she had repressed for years. After honestly facing her resentments, she saw her problem. Lucille surrendered her hidden hostility to God, and in a matter of weeks her depression disappeared.

Another Christian woman named Marcia is in her mid-thirties. She also was bothered by periods of depression. She said, "My depression almost carried me over the brink of sanity. When I was a small child my mother was too busy to give me much personal attention. And my father didn't show affection to any of his children. I needed love and attention very much because I was a sensitive child."

I began to get a picture of a timid and fragile little girl almost driven to despair by her busy mother and unloving father.

She continued: "When I didn't get any attention, I just clammed up tight. And because I didn't cry or anything, my mother thought I was happy. Mother spent her time with the other kids who cried more than I did. Even though I didn't cry outwardly, I was crying most of the time on the inside."

The results of the years of emotional starvation left a huge wound in Marcia's personality. She had buried her hurt deep within her and had driven it underground. The outcome of this repression was that Marcia found difficulty in accepting or giving love. She battled with imagined slights from her friends and her husband. Her becoming a Christian did not automatically repair the damage to her emotional life that she had suffered as a child. Not until several years after her conversion to Jesus Christ was she able to face her real problem and find healing in her deep mind.

Of course, not all emotional problems can be traced to one's parents; sometimes they develop in adult life. Sharon and B.J. had married just after they had been graduated from the state university. B.J. worked very hard, and he was determined to gain the material advantages he had missed as a child. But his hard work did not leave him much time to devote to Sharon. Sharon's father had not spent very much time with his family when Sharon was growing up, so when

Sharon married she expected her husband to spend a lot of time with her and take her hiking and boating.

When B.J. failed to give her the attention she wanted, Sharon became frustrated. Sharon and B.J. loved each other very much, and the last thing Sharon wanted to do was to nag or show any sign of disapproval. So for years she buried her resentments. These buried resentments produced headaches and backaches.

Finally, in a small prayer group, Sharon saw her problem. The others in her group prayed for her and helped her face her resentments. She surrendered these to God and talked them out with B.J. Only then was she able to get rid of her nagging headaches and backaches.

Sometimes situations outside the family play a part in stunting our emotional development. I remember my first few weeks in the first grade. I was the oldest child in our family, and going to the first grade was a completely new adventure for me. I looked forward to attending school on the first day, but I got off to a bad start.

On my way home for lunch, I met some older boys in the fourth and fifth grades who pushed me down several times and got my papers dirty. (I thought those papers with "Instructions to Parents" were as important as the Constitution of the United States.) The next day, on my way to school those same boys told me, "You might as well go back home, 'cause there ain't no school today."

I believed them and returned home. By the time my mother explained that they were joking, I was already tardy.

These boys harassed me for a long period of time, inventing a new sport each week. These events caused me to think something was wrong with me because the older boys didn't seem to like me. I worried constantly. However, I didn't tell my parents because I didn't want to be a sissy.

The experience was traumatic for me. I felt unworthy—almost guilty—because the older boys did not seem to like me. And for the first several years of my grade-school experience I drew into a semishell and developed an inferior feeling.

Many times we bring some of our personality problems on ourselves. For example, we deliberately do something which we know is wrong. This puts a sense of guilt upon us. Then we become afraid of being caught. Or we fear we may have to suffer the consequences of our wrongdoing. So fear rides piggyback on guilt. We push our uncomfortable feelings down into the unconscious mind and try to forget them.

But the guilt and fear remain dynamic even though we may no longer be conscious of them. We tend to bury our unpleasant feelings because we do not like to face them or deal with them. The mature Christian, however, has learned to take every difficult situation—including his damaged emotions—to Christ for forgiveness and healing.

Once in high school I stole a pair of scissors from the biology laboratory. I told myself that what I had done was not serious, and I soon forgot about it. But the knowledge of what I had done remained embedded in my deep mind. Years later, after I became a Christian, this theft surfaced one day as I was praying. It continued to appear in my consciousness as I tried to pray. I seemed to sense the Holy Spirit saying, "What about those scissors you stole? Don't you think you had better do something about them?"

I ignored the impression, but as the weeks passed, I became more and more uneasy. I found myself snapping at persons with whom I worked. I saw that I would find no peace unless I faced my wrongdoing and admitted my fault.

Finally, I wrote a letter to the high-school principal, enclosing some money to pay for the scissors. I also asked God to forgive me and to cleanse my memory of guilt. Then I felt clear about it, and I have never been bothered by that problem again. (I got a nice letter from the principal saying that all was well, and that he was deeply impressed by my confession.)

The unhealthy attitudes which we deposit in our unconscious minds act as a drag on us, and they tend to produce the infirmities which the New Testament speaks of. I believe that when we experience the blues or have an unaccountable sense of depression, it is because our unconscious mind is telling us that we need a deeper healing of God's grace.

Often the wounds of the deep mind are unknown to us because we have buried them below the conscious level. There they lurk and constitute an unnecessary burden until they are cleansed and healed.

Spiritual conversion to Jesus Christ does *not* automatically heal the personality wounds of the deep mind, any more than conversion cures a broken leg, or the mumps, or a common cold. The reason? Emotional scars are not in themselves sinful. They may be the *result* of sin, and they may become the *occasion* for sinning, but in themselves they are in the category of infirmities.

Jesus Christ was able to do all he did during the years of his incarnation in human flesh partly because he was a completely whole person. He was perfectly adjusted with his Father and with himself. He was totally free from infirmities of the spirit. His entire personality functioned harmoniously.

Unfortunately, none of us possesses the supreme composure and poise which Christ had.

Sometimes Christians who experience guilt, depression, and fear receive well-meaning but faulty advice. They may be told, "Your dedication to God is faulty—you're not fully consecrated to the Lord."

Or, occasionally persons are misled into thinking that all emotional problems should vanish at conversion. Believing that conversion is a magic cure-all, these Christians are distressed when they find that they still have problems after their conversion. When depression arises, for example, they may be tempted to say, "Well, I guess I wasn't converted after all."

While a lack of dedication to God *may* be the cause of guilt feelings and depression, frequently a different sort of problem lies at the root. The last piece of counsel a struggling Christian needs is, "You don't love God, so you might as well admit that you are not a Christian."

The writer to the Hebrews offered sound advice for struggling Christians. He said, ". . . do not throw away your confidence . . ." (Hebrews 10:35). That verse can be paraphrased, "Just because you experience a problem, don't surrender your faith in God. Hold on to your faith; God will help you through."

Even sincere and dedicated Christians are sometimes plagued by unhealed memories and repressed emotional needs. These memories, hurts, and attitudes need to be healed by God because we tend to make many of our decisions on the basis of our emotions. Perhaps most of us are motivated more by our feelings than our minds. And the unconscious part of us contains a veritable warehouse of emotions, many of which may be damaged.

Damaged emotions should not be confused with *original sin.* (Sin is certainly real enough, and it is a serious factor with which we must contend.) Damaged emotions result from our *acquired* tendencies and maladjustments.

Our impulses—healthy and unhealthy—are not able to think "right or wrong." Our impulses do not *reason* at all; they only *respond.* They clamor to be satisfied. They respond to *suggestion,* not logic. They do not care how their needs are met, just so long as they are met. This natural tendency is why damaged emotions can motivate us to sin if we are not delivered from their tyranny. The answer to damaged emotions and maladjusted complexes is not suppression. Rather, the solution is God's gracious work of healing.

How, then, can we be healed emotionally? What steps ought we to take in dealing with the problems of the deep mind? I have found these four suggestions very helpful: (1) realize you have an ally in the Holy Spirit, (2) recognize your real problem and face it, (3) relinquish the problem to Christ, (4) receive your healing.

First, realize you have an ally in the Holy Spirit. God sent the Holy Spirit into the world to help us. The purpose of the Holy Spirit is to make Christ's ministry real to us. Christ came to bring light to those of us who sit in darkness and to bring healing to our emotions as well as to our spirits and bodies. The Spirit communicates this ministry of Christ to us. His work is to build us up, not to tear us down.

The Holy Spirit is our friend and ally in showing us our deepest selves and our inner hurts. He does this not in order to condemn us, but to help us. The Holy Spirit ministers at the point of our deepest needs and our most troublesome infirmities. Matthew wrote about this ministry when he quoted Isaiah: " 'He took our infirmities and bore our diseases' " (Matthew 8:17).

Paul referred to the gracious work of the Spirit when he asserted, ". . . the Spirit helps us in our weaknesses; for we do not know how to pray as we ought, but the Spirit himself intercedes for us with sighs too deep for words" (Romans 8:26). The Holy Spirit actually intercedes for us in God's presence! ". . . God who knows the heart's secrets understands, of course, the Spirit's intention as he prays for those who love God" (Romans 8:27 PHILLIPS). The Spirit knows the secrets of our hearts—secrets which, as yet, we may not know about ourselves.

God can take the worst of us—even uptight neurotics— and bring emotional healing to us. He can create order out of inner chaos. Paul reassures us when he testifies to God's love: " 'My grace is enough for you: for where there is weakness, my power is shown the more completely' " (2 Corinthians 12:9 PHILLIPS).

The Holy Spirit uses many methods to show us our needs. Some of the more common avenues through which He speaks to us are:

—direct impressions.
—experience with our own failures.
—Scripture, sermons, and books.
—interpersonal relationships and dialogue with others.
—trained and sensitive Christian counselors.

Often God uses a combination of these ways to bring us deeper insights into our needs.

But remember this: The Holy Spirit is our friend and he wants to help us. The Holy Spirit brings God's unending love to us. He works gently and he always brings harmony, peace, and healing when we allow him.

Second, recognize your real problem and face it. It is not always easy to see where our emotional hurts began. Often they are rooted back in the distant past. But Christ is the Lord of time, and he can bring the past into our present consciousness. Or he can take us back in our memories to events which lie buried in our unconscious. The Spirit can overrule the time barrier. Peter reminds us: ". . . do not ignore this one fact, beloved, that with the Lord one day is as a thousand years, and a thousand years as one day" (2 Peter 3:8).

The uncovering of past wounds is good, not bad. Remembering some deep emotional wound of the past often becomes a necessary part of the healing process. Not everyone feels this way, however. One lady said to me that remembering past hurts was the "work of the devil," and that God never wanted us to recall unpleasant memories of the past. I think she was wrong. Her belief sounds similar to asserting that we ought to ignore weeds in the garden because they are unpleasant to think about.

To remember past emotional hurts can be the beginning of healing. Seeing one's problem in its true light is often a prelude to victory. If a memory is unhealed and if it festers within, we must have the courage to see it for what it is. Then we may more easily surrender our damaged emotions to God for his healing.

One young woman had some deeply repressed bitterness, and her buried hostility caused her to be moody. Her friends did not understand her problem of buried resentments and she lost several jobs because of her attitudes. Then she began to pray about her problem, and the Holy Spirit began to uncover the bitterness she was carrying. She was well on the way to the healing of her attitudes.

Then she told some friends about the self-insights she was gaining. Unfortunately, they immediately advised her, "That's the work of the devil. You are demon-possessed to think of such things." They forced her to kneel while they laid hands on her and prayed for the casting out of demons. (By the way, in the New Testament, Jesus *never* laid hands on anyone when casting out demons.)

The actions of her well-meaning friends only confused her and compounded her problem. They had mistakenly ascribed the work of the Holy Spirit to the work of demons! She later found a Christian counselor who helped her to see that she was not possessed with demons at all. He led her to pray for the healing of her deep resentments. God healed her emotions, and now she is a radiant Christian woman.

Facing one's problem requires a deep honesty and an openness to God. It requires a willingness to say, "I was wrong to react as I did." Often *we* are more to blame than our circumstances, and we need to admit our own failures.

Facing our problem of unhealed memories also means that we must ask ourselves the question, "Do I really want to be healed?" Some persons actually enjoy their emotional problems because they like the attention their neuroticism brings to them. Others prefer to suffer deep resentments and fears rather than face their own responsibility.

So, ask God to show you your problem. Insights gained can become the beginning of your healing.

Third, relinquish your problem to Christ. About ten years after my conversion to Christ, I began to be aware of a sense of anxiety which was developing in me. Moreover, I got impatient when things didn't move as quickly as I thought they should. I prayed about my problem, but I seemed to be making little headway.

Finally, I asked myself, "When did I begin to feel unhappy? When did a cloud come over me?" I began to realize that none of us can analyze his own problems without the help of the Holy Spirit. So I asked God to show me the source of my anxiety.

In prayer, I gradually sensed that my particular problem had really begun over twenty years before. Even though I had since become a Christian, I hadn't accepted God's forgiveness in a certain area of my life. I was carrying guilt for something I had done as a child. As I look back, I see that what I did was actually only a minor sin. But I had buried it for over twenty years, and it had continued to plague my unconscious mind. Even though I had become a Christian, it was still there.

I surrendered it to Christ. I prayed something like this: "God, with your help I see myself as a small boy. I see that you were beside me all the time even though I didn't know you. I see now that you loved me, even though I wasn't aware of it. I accept your forgiveness now. I receive your healing of the guilt I have been carrying all these years." God healed that part of my memory which needed his touch. And it was as real a healing as if I had been physically healed of tonsilitis.

The Holy Spirit is a divine psychiatrist. He gently reveals to us our damaged emotions, and he also offers his healing.

An acquaintance named Sam told me how he had gone to a counselor for a number of sessions. Sam and his counselor discussed the matter of guilt. The counselor said, "We all sin as you have done." (He was right here.) Then he went on to say, "But don't let sin bother you. Sin is a doctrine of the church and it is altogether outmoded—it's an old-fashioned belief. All morality is relative. Just forget about your 'sins.' "

Later, Sam said, "He uncovered the problem which was bothering me all right, but he turned right around and told me to bury it again. I finally faced squarely what was troubling me and I asked God to cleanse my memories. God healed me. Now when I remember the past I do not feel guilty; I just thank God that I've been healed."

I know a couple with four children. The wife has some real emotional problems which cause her to be moody. Her husband is no help, for he gives her poor advice. At least three or four times a day, he says, "Nancy, snap out of it." However, if Nancy could snap out of it by herself she would have done so long ago. She is powerless. Her husband might as well say, "Nancy, go to the world series and pitch a no-hit game."

Another bit of bad advice is: "It really isn't so bad; don't worry. Your problem will go away by itself." Or another piece of poor counsel: "You just think you have a problem; it's all in your imagination."

Damaged emotions and unhealed memories cannot be overcome by denying their existence or by the sheer effort of personal willpower. They require a touch from God before spiritual health can be restored. Only when we become willing to relinquish our problem to Christ and allow him to heal us, can we be made whole.

Fourth, receive your healing from God. See Jesus by your side. Accept his love. Know as the Psalmist did: ". . . he restores my soul" (Psalms 23:3).

Relax. Don't hurry. Wait patiently in God's healing presence; don't try to force things. Be still before God. Don't struggle. Don't strive. Just quietly let the Holy Spirit help you surrender your hurt to God. Let him help you receive your deliverance.

Sometimes God heals instantly; sometimes he heals over a period of time. Gradual healing is not the result of God's reluctance. Rather, God heals gradually because he knows our unconscious minds tend to respond slowly. Don't let feelings and impressions govern you. Like all other good gifts from God, the healing of the emotions comes through *faith.* Trust God to deliver you in his own way and in his own time.

Even when healing is gradual, there is usually a breakthrough, a beginning point when you receive by faith God's healing power. As you pray, picture yourself as whole and as liberated by God's power. This is not auto-suggestion. It is the beginning of faith. Real faith *sees* and accepts in advance what it asks for.

Just how God heals, none of us really understands. But this much we do know: *God does heal!* The Holy Spirit helps our infirmities and renews our "inner man." God's love is without bounds—it is not restricted in any way. It reaches all the way to our deepest inner needs where the hurt is the greatest. And there—down in the wounded emotions and the painful memories—God imparts his healing love and makes men whole.

4

Ignorance Is Not Bliss

DURING A FELLOWSHIP meal in a large interracial church, I sat across the table from a cultured and well-dressed woman. In the course of her remarks, she was discussing miracles. She said, "Jesus performed many miracles. For example, you all remember the passage in the New Testament that tells of the time Jesus took eighteen white stones and turned them into eighteen white doves."

Of course there is no such passage in the Bible. Apparently she heard the story from someone who heard the story from someone else who heard it from some other person. Whatever the original version may have been, it was distorted greatly in the transmission.

Oral tradition forms the basis of a surprising amount of our thinking. Many persons rely a great deal on hearsay and rumor, and therefore an amazing amount of religious ignorance thrives among otherwise intelligent persons. And even some Christians entertain curious and bizarre religious notions that have no biblical basis, at times uncritically accepting superstition and myth.

In matters of religion, however, ignorance is *not* bliss. Ignorance about Christ and his way produces ineffective Christian discipleship. Jesus told us to worship God with our *minds* as well as our hearts because our thinking forms the basis of our acting. Religious ignorance is anything but bliss because it usually results in defeated and anemic Christians.

Much religious ignorance is perpetuated by our sectarian and denominational traditions. Christ found it so in his day. He asked certain religious leaders, ". . . why do you transgress the commandment of God for the sake of your tradition?" (Matthew 15:3). Man's tendency to follow custom rather than God prompted Paul to write, "Be on your guard; do not let your minds be captured by hollow and delusive speculations, based on traditions of man-made teaching . . . and not on Christ" (Colossians 2:8 NEB).

The only proper alternative for our traditions is Jesus Christ himself. Thomas was one of Jesus' closest followers, yet at times he was skeptical and hard to convince. On one occasion he asked Jesus, "Lord, we do not know where you are going; how can we know the way?"

Jesus responded, "I am the way, and the truth, and the life . . ." (John 14:5,6).

Christ was saying, "If you're following me, you're already following the truth." Christ could say that, because he is God's supreme revelation.

But how can a contemporary Christian know if he is really following Christ? How can any of us be sure that we have not allowed the barnacles of human tradition to attach themselves to the truth and obscure it?

In my own life, I have had to overcome some false understandings of Christian discipleship. I was not able to make much progress on the route of Christian maturity until I abandoned certain religious conventions which were simply not true. I discovered three tests of Christian truth. These are: *Scripture, real life,* and *the context of total truth.*

The Bible constitutes the Christian's source book; it shapes his thinking and acting. Any religious teaching which is completely novel and foreign to biblical principles should glare like a red traffic light to the Christian.

Of course, the Bible does not in every case give specific answers to specific questions. For example the Bible does not give any direct advice on church schools, tobacco, birth control, or urban problems. However, the Bible does contain *principles* which can be applied to every circumstance. And it is the Christian's responsibility to be completely familiar with the spirit and principles of Scripture.

The Bible pulses with unique authority; it displays an amazing relevance to today's world. The New Testament was written by men who knew Christ personally or by those to whom Christ personally appeared after his ascension. Some of the writers walked closely with Christ for over three years. All of the writers were especially inspired by the Holy Spirit as they wrote.

Any teaching about Christian discipleship which is valid will coincide with the Bible. And those teachings which are contradictory to the Bible must be rejected. Of course, we can always gain help from books other than the Bible. But the Bible is the Christian's *basic* source for religious truth and the final touchstone for Christian doctrine.

I also learned quite early in my Christian life that if a teaching about the Christian life were true, it would work in daily life. Some teachings which are urged on Christians are ineffective in the rough-and-tumble of the marketplace. Christian teaching is above all else very livable. It works. And it will prove itself in the context of practical living.

I once heard a speaker say, "If you really have the fullness of the Holy Spirit you can be sure of two things: First, you won't ever have any sexual temptations, and second, you will never have your feelings hurt no matter how much slander and falsehood are spread about you."

I am afraid that these high-sounding words are just not true! Certainly, one can receive God's deliverance from sexual impurity and from a vindictive spirit. But it is unrealistic to expect to be spared from the temptations which are common to our humanity.

The religion of Jesus Christ is no mystical, armchair religion, nor is it mere theory. It is intensely practical! It really works in the home and at the shop—and during those times when our whole world seems to tumble in. If a teaching about the Christian life is not workable and livable, it is not true.

One other test: Every teaching about the Christian life should be judged in the light of the whole body of truth. Error usually includes elements of the truth; but a portion of truth separated from the whole is exceedingly dangerous. Two half-truths never constitute a whole truth.

Most of us find it hard to see both sides of an issue. We discover a certain truth; the discovery proves exciting to us. But in our zeal, we sometimes forget the other side of the coin. We emphasize one truth to the neglect of a complementary truth. And sloppy thinking of this sort breeds heresy.

Paul lamented a lopsided understanding of the truth in the Corinthian church. Some of the Christians were banding together in the "Paul party"; others withdrew into the "Peter party." Still others followed the way of the "Apollos party."

Paul strenuously objected to such sectarianism. He

stressed that a party spirit usually results in a partial and incomplete Christianity. Paul instructed the immature Christians at Corinth to follow Christ, not a party within the church. He wrote, ". . . all things are yours . . . and you are Christ's" (1 Corinthians 3:21–23). He was saying, "You don't belong to a party in the church; you belong to Christ. And belonging to Christ, everything belongs to you."

So, these tests—Scripture, real life, and the context of total truth—are realistic and workable screens through which all religious truth must pass.

Of course, everyone's experiences are different. No two Christians have exactly the same pilgrimage. None of us apprehends truth or is apprehended by truth in precisely the same manner.

Four colossal misconceptions clouded my understanding of Christian discipleship during my early months of following Christ. First, I thought that only ministers could ever be first-class Christians. Second, I thought that Christians were not supposed to enjoy nonspiritual things. Third, I thought that the Christian life was essentially obedience to a set of rules. And fourth, I thought that success in the Christian life depended on how hard I worked to be a good Christian. All of these are gross misunderstandings of Christianity. Some of them were communicated to me by well-meaning Christian "advisors," and some of them I thought up myself.

Each of these negative ideas can be restated in a positive and constructive fashion: (1) Every Christian is called to be a first-class Christian; (2) Christ blessed every area of human life; (3) Christian disciples are under grace, not law; and (4) The Christian life is lived in the power of the Holy Spirit.

First, every Christian is called to be a first-class Christian.

After I became a Christian, I immediately developed an enormous interest in the Bible; I read it with great enthusiasm. The Bible had not always held such a fascination for me. For years it had been as dry as yesterday morning's unbuttered toast. But after I was converted, Scripture came alive to me. The words on each page often seemed to leap out at me in neon letters.

I made some life-changing discoveries as I read. One of the first new insights which came to me was in the Book of Romans. In part, the opening verses read, "Paul, a servant of Jesus Christ. . . .To all that be in Rome, beloved of God, called to be saints . . ." (Romans 1:1,7 KJV). From this I asked myself the question: "If *all* the Roman Christians were called to be saints, does this also mean that all Christians today are called to be saints?"

As I looked further into the New Testament, I concluded that the answer to this question is yes. God has called all followers of Christ to be saints, laymen as well as clergymen.

Without distinction, the New Testament analogies of the church include each Christian as a member of the Body of Christ. All Christians are "stones" in a building, "members" of a body, "branches" in a vine. Every Christian has the same calling: a calling to sainthood!

To be sure, each Christian has a different task and a different function. But each Christian has equal importance in the church. There are no second-class citizens in the Kingdom of God—all are first-class citizens. Paul writes, ". . . some should be apostles, some prophets, some evangelists, some pastors and teachers, for the equipment of the saints [and remember every Christian is a saint], for the work of ministry, for building up the body of Christ [the church] . . ." (Ephesians 4:11,12).

The meaning? Every Christian is a minister and a first-class one at that.

Early in the second century, the notion developed that the laying on of hands conferred a special authority and power to the clergy. Soon it was commonly accepted (tradition again!) that the clergymen were especially holy because they were connected back to the apostles through ordination to the priesthood. This belief was called apostolic succession, and some Christians even today insist this rite confers special powers to the clergy.

The development of a special class called the priesthood led to the evolution of two classes of Christians. The higher class consisted of the clergy; the lower class was made up of ordinary laymen. During the Middle Ages the notion developed that the church was rooted in the ministry, and without the ministry no salvation was possible. The ministry became a self-perpetuating oligarchy within the church.

In only a short time the idea emerged that celibacy was a higher state of holiness than the married state. One tradition was added to another until the laymen ultimately became spectators in the church, watching the clergy perform their ministerial functions. Laymen were relegated to second-class membership within the Kingdom of God. The entire development was completely foreign to the spirit and practice of the New Testament.

This unfortunate development does not imply that we ought to dispense with clergymen in the church. We need them badly! But it does point to the error of regarding clergymen as a special class of Christians who are more holy than the nonclerical Christians. Ministers are not qualitatively superior to laymen. They serve the church in a special *function*, but not because they have powers denied to laymen.

Each Christian is a disciple of Christ and God calls him to his own unique style of ministry. While all Christians are not called to preach, all are expected to be saints and to manifest the fruit of the Spirit. One of the most hopeful and exciting trends in the contemporary church is that the laymen are awakening from a centuries-old slumber. They are coming alive—alive to their calling in the gospel, alive to their role as Christians called to be saints. Today, the Holy Spirit is thawing out a vast army of laymen to do God's work in the world.

Laymen are discovering that they must not depend on a single sermon once a week to nourish them spiritually. Good sermons are helpful, of course. But contemporary laymen are beginning to realize that mature disciples of Jesus Christ must learn how to feed themselves spiritually each day. Effective Christian discipleship hinges on regular communion with Christ, accompanied by obedience to him in the affairs of daily life.

The same requisites also apply to clergymen. The spiritually vital minister knows that he cannot rest on his ordination. He understands that he is subject to the same spiritual laws as the layman, and he is not exempt from prayer just because he is always doing God's work. In fact, the day is past when a minister can automatically gain a hearing just because he is a minister. Nothing less than the power of the Holy Spirit will suffice to give him a valid ministry.

No class distinction exists among Christ's disciples. All are called to become first-class Christians in God's Kingdom.

Second, Christ blessed every area of human life. During

the first several weeks following my conversion to Jesus Christ I received a barrage of well-meaning advice. Some of my new friends advised me, "Ken, now that you are a Christian you must leave all the worldly things behind you. You mustn't engage in nonreligious activities. You must do only spiritual things."

I'm sure this advice was well meant. But problems arose when it came to deciding what was worldly and what was spiritual.

There can be no doubt that the New Testament urges a separated life for the Christian. Paul advises, "Don't let the world around you squeeze you into its own mold, but let God remold your minds from within . . ." (Romans 12:2 PHILLIPS).

But my thinking was clouded on three counts: First, I understood the phrase, "don't be conformed to," to mean "don't be in contact with. . . ." Second, I gained the impressions from some friends that right and wrong could be determined by a set of rules. (Several persons suggested to me a list of worldly things as long as this page. Their list forbade cosmetics for the ladies, colorful clothes for the men, and movies for everybody.) And, third, I was introduced to a negativism which seemed to me to be contrary to the positive thrust of the gospel.

I do not judge these persons, nor do I have the slightest doubt about their sincerity and their Christian commitment. But even though they were earnest, I don't believe they were right.

I read some books and heard some sermons which supported the advice of my friends. Some writers and speakers even went so far as to suggest (tacitly if not overtly) that our bodies are tainted with sin and that only our "spirits" are good. This notion is a reversion to the ancient heresy of gnosticism which viewed the human body as a source of evil. Certainly, to view the body and its appetites as evil is to ignore the fact that God created us as we are. If I were going to pick a "mistake" that God made in creation I would personally prefer to nominate mosquitoes rather than the human body!

An underlying motif of these Christians is that disciples ought not to enjoy themselves too much. Perhaps a fitting motto for them would be: "Soberness is next to godliness."

As a new Christian, I took seriously all the advice I received. Now that I look back, I see that I was naive and uncritical. But even then as I reflected on what these spiritual advisors were saying, I felt very uncomfortable with some of the negatives which dominated their point of view. I did not know why, but these ideas did not seem to fit. I felt like David in Saul's armor.

My apprehension gradually turned into a loss of joy and the birth of a critical spirit toward other Christians who did not follow the letter of the law as I was trying to do. In my early attempts to witness to others about my newfound faith, I'm afraid that sometimes I was more interested in my own performance than in Christ. I turned off some of my friends completely. I thought I was being persecuted.

However, I was not being persecuted at all. I was just demonstrating more than my share of stupidity. I was trying to foist off on my non-Christian friends a secondhand set of rules rather than a living and vital Christ.

Naturally I was not winning many people to Christ and I was fast losing the thrill of being a Christian. I did not understand that all of life had been sanctified by Christ. I failed to see that Christ made no distinction between the sacred and the secular, although he did distinguish between *sinful* and *righteous*. Christ was interested in transforming all of my life, not in removing me from large portions of life.

One day, as I was reading in the Book of Genesis, I discovered what was for me a new verse: "And God saw every thing that he had made, and, behold, it was very good" (Genesis 1:31). I read and reread the verse. Slowly, it dawned on me that "every thing" meant *everything*. God's creation is good. The psalmist expressed it this way: "The earth is the LORD'S, and the fulness thereof . . . " (Psalm 24:1). I saw that sin does not reside in *things;* sin stems from our *attitudes*.

As I read on, I came to the story of Adam and Eve's temptation and disobedience. There was no chemical in the forbidden fruit which got Eve into trouble. God could just as well have designated some other piece of fruit. It was not the fruit that wrought the havoc of sin—it was disobedience to God's Word.

Then I remembered how Christ joyously participated in the wedding feast at Cana and even provided the very best wine for the occasion. I remembered how he loved good conversation with others—Mary, Zaccheus, Nicodemus, the woman at the well. Christ's love did not allow him to separate himself from contact with real life. He associated with "good" men and "bad" men alike. Separation and withdrawal were the ways of the Pharisees, but not the ways of Christ.

I reread Paul's statement, ". . . all things are yours . . ." (1 Corinthians 3:21) and I began to see that Christ wanted me to participate in life and to enjoy his good gifts fully.

Finally I learned to make my own decisions about what I

should do as a Christian, even if it meant going against the advice of my well-meaning friends. After all, no set of rules can possibly cover all aspects of the Christian's life.

When trying to determine whether a course of action is right, and when there is no definite scriptural teaching to cover the issue, the Christian asks a simple question: "Will this harm my relationship with God?" Or better still: "Will this help me worship Christ better and will it renew my body, mind, and spirit, without causing a weaker brother to stumble?"

Christ blessed every area of human life. God ". . . richly furnishes us with everything to enjoy" (1 Timothy 6:17). No sincerely dedicated Christian disciple would want to refuse God's provision for his enrichment, nor would he want to pervert these provisions into sin.

Christian conduct cannot be regulated by the most narrow views held by the most conservative Christians. There are times when one must do what he thinks is right, even if others are not in agreement with him.

Third, Christian disciples are under grace, not law. For me, learning the meaning of *grace* was a slow process. I am still learning, in fact. And the more I learn the more I stand in wonder at God's love, for there seems to be something deeply embedded within each one of us which prompts: "Earn your own way." From early childhood, many of us have been taught; "Lift your own share of the weight." We are conditioned to believe that we can expect only what we earn by our own prowess and energy, and most of us are not conditioned to take anything we do not merit.

Before I was converted to Christ, I thought that religion

consisted of obedience to the law. Obedience to the law of the church—the laws of the Bible—the law of human decency. But living under the law constitutes the very heart of earning one's favor with God. And Christians are not under the law; they are under grace. The Christian way stands in antithesis to human merit and man's worthiness before God.

One of the ABCs of the gospel is that man must rely totally upon God's undeserved love and not upon his own righteousness. "For it is by his grace you are saved, through trusting him; it is not your own doing. It is God's gift, not a reward for work done. There is nothing for anyone to boast of" (Ephesians 2:8,9 NEB). From start to finish, the Christian life is based on the grace of God; it is not dependent upon man's powers or his personal achievements.

After my conversion, when I started reading the Bible, I read it with colored glasses. That is, I read it with certain preconceived ideas as to what it would say. So, when I read, I looked for rules to obey and for regulations to follow. I thought that the Christian life should be approached through a number of precepts and laws. I believed that being a good Christian depended on how well I followed these rules.

But the Christian life is not based on *law;* it is based on *grace.* Law presupposes a certain amount of fear, and it emphasizes duty. But grace implies love and gratitude; under grace, the Christian serves from devotion, not duty. Law suggests human merit; grace speaks *divine mercy.* Law brings bondage; grace issues in freedom. In short, law advances human endeavor, and *man* becomes the focus of attention. But grace flows from divine activity, and allows God to occupy the central place.

The Christian disciple is not committed to a *principle,* but to a *person.* That person is, of course, Jesus Christ. Principles are impersonal and cannot produce a Christlike character. But Christ meets us person-to-person, just where we are. He evokes a response from us which no precept possibly can.

I found that when I committed myself to the rules which I squeezed out of the Bible, I was becoming a *legalist.* Legalists slavishly follow laws; they have little joy, and they are often intolerant of the performance of others. I found myself edging steadily into the very same trap which had snared the Pharisees centuries ago.

By way of contrast, I had a friend named Arnie who made quite a different mistake. He committed himself to a principle also, but his was the principle of *freedom.* Whereas I was getting ensnared in the ropes of legalism, Arnie was cutting himself loose from all restraints in the name of freedom.

Arnie's reasoning was, "Since I'm not saved by my works anyway, it doesn't matter how I live. I can sin if I want to, because I'm free forever from the demands of the law." Arnie wasn't committed to the person of Chirst; he was committed to the principle of freedom. Arnie explained it to me this way: "God freely forgives sinners; so the more I sin, the more he can forgive."

Paul encountered such Christians, and he couched his response in strong language: "Shall we sin to our heart's content and see how far we can exploit the grace of God? What a ghastly thought!" (Romans 6:1,2 PHILLIPS).

I was wrong . . . Arnie was wrong. Both of us were following concepts rather than Christ.

Through the help of a couple of good books and some mature Christian friends I met, Christ freed me from the bondage of the law. I realized what Paul meant when he wrote, ". . . you are not under law but under grace" (Romans 6:14).

It was then that I began to understand that the Christian's salvation does not depend upon the demands of the law, but at the same time he is bound by love to be a follower of Christ. This new understanding liberated me from encroaching legalism which would have stifled my Christian life and hopelessly dwarfed my spiritual growth. Christians who are living under grace serve God not because they *have* to; they serve because they *want* to and because they are *enabled* to.

As I began to grasp the meaning of grace, I was led quite naturally to another discovery about Christian discipleship.

Fourth, the Christian life is lived in the power of the Holy Spirit. My error in viewing discipleship as obedience to laws was accompanied by another equally false notion. I believed that my success as a Christian depended on how hard I worked at it. I had never stopped to think it through, but I was acting on the following formula: "Christ forgives me and imparts his new life to me; and after that, it's pretty much up to me."

Mine was a fairly common perspective. Most new Christians are overjoyed with their new life in Christ. Their first impulse is to determine to serve him faithfully. The typical prayer of a new Christian runs something like this: "Lord, I'm so grateful for your salvation that I'm going to do many things for you. I'm going to do this—and do that—I'm going to be a model Christian."

That is a sincere prayer, to be sure. But it contains a major flaw: the overuse of the pronoun *"I." "I'm* going to do such-and-such. . . ." The typical new Christian has a great confidence in his own ability to serve Christ, and so he sets out on his own to be a good Christian. That's what I did, and I soon ran headlong into difficulties too big for me to handle.

After about eight months of up-and-down discipleship, I began to see that I didn't have an ounce of power within myself to live the Christian life. But I saw that Christ doesn't ask us to be his disciples in our own strength. He wants to live in us through the Holy Spirit.

I'll admit that sounds a bit mystical. And I'm certainly not suggesting that our personalities are obliterated or canceled out. God does not want robots who are less than human. He wants us freely to serve him with our entire personalities. But in order to do this we need the inward dynamic of the Holy Spirit.

Paul expressed the union of Christ and disciple in a classic way: "I have been crucified with Christ; it is no longer I who live, but Christ who lives in me; and the life I now live in the flesh I live by faith in the Son of God, who loved me and gave himself for me" (Galatians 2:20). The Christian still lives, yet it is Christ who lives in him.

How can Christ live in every Christian? Only one way: through the person of the Holy Spirit. This is why Jesus spent so many of his last hours with his disciples teaching them about the Spirit's ministry.

Almost all of the victorious Christians I have met tell me a similar story. Nearly all of them say that it took them a period of time after their conversion before they learned by sad experience how spiritually powerless they were in themselves. Only after they came to see their own weakness were they able to see their need of God's Spirit to make them adequate.

We usually ask God only for the things we sense that we need. Only after we learn how weak we really are do Christ's promises of the Spirit's power seem important to us.

No, ignorance is not bliss. But Christians do not have to remain uncertain of God's plan for them. Remember the promise: "If any of you lacks wisdom, let him ask God, who gives to all men generously and without reproaching, and it will be given him" (James 1:5).

Ask God to help you, and he will. He stands ready to give you all the wisdom you need.

5

Locked Closets
And Unavailable Keys

THE EXCESS BAGGAGE of maladjusted emotions and the *un-blissful* ignorance of discipleship are not the only issues facing the Christian. He faces still another significant problem: his own self-will.

I found that when I became a Christian I had a deep love for God, but my desire to have things my own way did not automatically vanish. I wanted to do God's will, certainly, but I wanted my own way as well. I found an inner conflict—a struggle between what I wanted and what I knew God wanted. Paul's dilemma seemed to describe my own situation perfectly: "My own behavior baffles me. For I find myself not doing what I really want to do but doing what I really loathe" (Romans 7:15 PHILLIPS).

I wondered at times if I really was converted after all. I studied the Bible and tried to find out what it meant to be converted. I looked up biblical references to the word *saved*. I found the word used with reference to the past, the present, and the future. In some places the Bible says that Christians *have been saved*. In other places Scripture records that Christians *are being saved*. And in still other places I read that Christians *shall be saved*. Our salvation relates to what we have been, what we are, and what we shall be.

A number of my Christian friends talked about having been saved. But I heard very little about the continuing process of *being* saved. I wondered what the Bible writers meant when they wrote about the ongoing process of salvation. Fortunately, I found a great deal of help from the Apostle Paul. He wrote that Christians ". . . are being changed into [Christ's] likeness from one degree of glory to another; for this comes from the Lord who is the Spirit" (2 Corinthians 3:18).

Then two ideas began to evolve in my thinking. First, we are not as completely changed at conversion as we ultimately will be. That is, God's work in the Christian does not end as soon as he becomes a disciple of Christ. To be sure, a definite change begins at conversion: ". . . if a man is in Christ he becomes a new person altogether—the past is finished and gone, everything has become fresh and new" (2 Corinthians 5:17 PHILLIPS). But we are not as spiritually mature as God wants us to be. Spiritual transformation is a lifetime process.

A second idea I began to grasp was that the crucial yes which I said to God at the time of my conversion was not the end of my yes-saying. It is somewhat like marriage. One says a determinative "I do" at the time of the marriage ceremony, but that is not the end of the matter. Marriage is a lifetime relationship with one's marriage partner. Likewise, Christianity is a lifetime relationship with Jesus Christ.

Growing Christians continue to find new areas of their lives which need to be converted. Most Christians have little compartments in their lives which have been airtight and which as yet Christ has not gotten into.

Maybe the problem is a wrong attitude toward other races, a wrong attitude toward money, a wrong attitude toward business. One man said that he had been a Christian for two years before his wallet became converted! Many Christians have been truly changed by Jesus Christ, but they still have some locked closets in their lives. And, as yet, the keys to these closets are unavailable to Christ.

Locked closets and unavailable keys: the reason many Christians fail to grow spiritually. Often Christians are not aware that they have some closets which have not been Christianized.

But Christ is very faithful and patient. He lovingly reveals unconverted attitudes which linger in the Christian. He stands at the door and knocks, seeking entrance into those dark closets. The maturing Christian willingly surrenders these locked closets to Christ. As he does so, he grows in his relationship to God. He continues to experience joy as he walks with Christ.

But what if a Christian refuses to surrender a key to Christ?

If he persists in resisting Christ's will, he backslides. Backsliding is not failing to live a perfect life; it is stubbornly refusing to surrender all of one's life to Christ. It is keeping certain closets in the heart reserved for self alone.

Bill came to a small prayer group to which I belong. He was heavy with a sense of despair. Bill was fearful that he had backslidden and he wondered if he had lost his salvation.

Bill had lied at work in order to cover up a mistake he had made. He had forgotten to put the company car in the company garage after using it. The next morning, the boss found the car in front of the office where Bill had left it, key still intact. The boss was furious and asked him if he had used the car. Bill said, "Not me."

Bill asked the members of our prayer group if he had backslidden. He wondered if he were still a Christian.

Together, our group read 1 John. We studied such verses as: ". . . if we freely admit that we have sinned, we find God utterly reliable and straightforward—he forgives our sins and makes us thoroughly clean from all that is evil." ". . . if a man should sin, remember that our advocate before the Father is Jesus Christ the righteous, the one who made personal atonement for our sins . . ." (1 John 1:9 and 2:1,2 PHILLIPS).

From these verses and others, we concluded that a *single sin* rarely ever constitutes backsliding. When one sins and is greatly troubled that he has offended God, his very concern indicates that he has probably not backslidden. He is bothered about offending God, and this is a very good sign indeed.

God is infinitely more patient with us than we can imagine. His compassionate heart moves out toward us in unfathomable love. He desires to forgive us. All he wants us to do is to confess our sin to him and allow him to pardon us. In fact, Christ takes the divine initiative in seeking us out and calling us to restored fellowship.

An incident in Peter's life illustrates Christ's concern. Peter sinned and denied his Lord, but Christ came seeking him. "Just as day was breaking, Jesus stood on the beach; yet the disciples did not know that it was Jesus" (John 21:4). (Often we are unaware at first of Christ's standing beside us seeking renewed fellowship.) Jesus immediately began to restore the blurred fellowship between him and Peter.

God's initiative can also be seen in the Garden of Eden. After Adam and Eve sinned, they ". . . hid themselves from the presence of the LORD God among the trees of the garden" (Genesis 3:8). It was God who sought them out. The account reads: ". . . the LORD God called to the man, and said to him, 'where are you?' " (Genesis 3:9). God took the first step to renew a broken fellowship.

Whenever man's strained relationship with God is restored, two elements are always present: personal recognition of one's wrongdoing, and confession to God. As soon as we acknowledge our wrongdoing, God forgives!

What then is backsliding? Backsliding occurs when we *consciously* and *knowingly* turn from Jesus Christ and settle down into a regular pattern of disobedience. When we confirm a broken relationship with God as normative, we backslide.

What causes one to backslide? Backsliding does not normally happen all at once, any more than ruined marriages develop overnight. Usually one gradually moves further and further from Christ. As a rule, one does not suddenly decide to turn from Christ. Backsliding ordinarily results from a long series of small acts on our part; the further we get from Christ, the cooler our attitude becomes. Backsliding stems from consistently having one's own way and refusing to consider Christ's will.

Thus, unsurrendered areas of one's life may be compared to locked closets and unavailable keys. A locked closet is reserving a certain part of our lives for ourselves, and we cling to the key when we do not allow Christ access.

Christians cannot backslide without being aware of it. The Holy Spirit gently speaks to the Christian again and again before he backslides. God is more interested in our Christian life than we are ourselves.

Why do we persist in stubbornly holding onto the keys to certain closets in our hearts? That, of course, is the riddle of the ages. Why we Christians at times persist in keeping part of our lives from Christ is difficult to comprehend.

Our basic problem seems to be that we put ourselves before God. We place self-interests before a concern for God's will for us. God is Creator of the universe and has every right to set the ground rules for man. The very revealing of his will to us is an act of his concern and love.

Part of God's plan for the human family is that he has given to man a certain amount of freedom and responsibility. God took a risk in giving man this freedom. But it was a risk God was willing to take because he desires man's freely-given response of love and service. God never forces discipleship on anyone. Man has the ability to turn from God and to disobey him; he also has the ability to receive God's grace.

No matter how seriously the Christian may disobey God, God always offers restored fellowship. In the early days of the Hebrew nation, God's message was: ". . . I have set before you life and death, blessing and curse; therefore choose life, that you and your descendants may live . . ." (Deuteronomy 30:- 19). God holds the same attitude toward us today.

Because of man's natural tendency to make sinful choices, he is unable to make good choices without God's help. Paul wrote: ". . . it is God who is at work within you, giving you the will and the power to achieve his purpose" (Philippians 2:13 PHILLIPS). Yet, man must cooperate with God's grace by choosing to accept his help.

By no means does our salvation depend on *our ability;* it depends on *God's faithfulness.* But man's ability and his responsibility are two different things. We have a responsibility to continue to receive God's love into our lives. One apostle put it this way: ". . . keep yourselves in the love of God . . ." (Jude v. 21). And Jesus put it even more strongly: "Why do you call me 'Lord, Lord,' and not do what I tell you?" (Luke 6:46).

The Lord told a parable of a wise man who built on the rock and a foolish man who built upon sand. When the rain, the floods, and the winds came, only the house on the rock remained. Jesus said, ". . . every one who hears these words of mine and does not do them will be like a foolish man who built his house upon the sand . . . and it fell; and great was the fall of it" (Matthew 7:26,27).

Backsliding comes from a failure to obey Christ's word. His word is not an unpleasant demand which the Christian must fulfill. It is a joy which the Christian regards as a privilege. An ancient worshiper of God declared, ". . . thy law is my delight" (Psalms 119:77).

But what about Christians who have broken their fellowship with God? Does God still love them? Of course he does! Can fallen Christians be restored to fellowship with God? Certainly!

Then how?

Three things are necessary in restoring a broken relationship with God: (1) confess your sin, (2) forsake your sin, and (3) walk in renewed obedience to Christ.

Confession of sin strikes a blow at our pride. But confession of guilt is much better than suppression of guilt. Pretending to others and to ourselves that we are not responsible for our sins solves nothing. God knows about our sins; confession to him is our wisest course of action.

Confession implies that we recognize that we have

offended God and that we are responsible for the resulting disrupted relationship. We need not try to blame others. For, in the final analysis, we alone are accountable for our sins. The fault lies with ourselves; we fool no one when we deny it.

You may be saying, "But you don't know how difficult my temptation was. No one could have faced the temptations I had." A Christian who had fallen into a sexual sin said: "The circumstances were such that it was impossible to resist. Anyone with red blood in his veins would have done the same."

Anyone? What about Joseph? (Read the interesting story in Genesis 39:6–12.)

When we succumb to temptation, we have no one to blame but ourselves. "No temptation has come your way that is too hard for flesh and blood to bear. But God can be trusted not to allow you to suffer any temptation beyond your powers of endurance. He will see to it that every temptation has a way out, so that it will never be impossible for you to bear it" (1 Corinthians 10:13 PHILLIPS).

David the psalmist described an experience which he had because his sin had disrupted his relationship with God:

> When I declared not my sin, my
>   body wasted away
>   through my groaning all day
>   long.
> For day and night thy hand was
>   heavy upon me;
>   my strength was dried up as by
>   the heat of summer.

> I acknowledged my sin to thee,
>   and I did not hide my iniquity;
> I said, "I will confess my transgres-
>   sions to the Lord";
>   then thou didst forgive the guilt of
>   my sin.
>
>   Psalms 32:3–5

Notice that when David refused to confess his sin he was in mental, spiritual and physical agony. (Unconfessed sin can actually cause physical illness.) But when he confessed his sin to God, God forgave him and healed his troubled spirit.

Luke, the writer of Acts, described a revival which took place at Ephesus. Paul was there, and he preached daily in the synagogue for three months (Acts 19:8). But it was really a lay revival. The revival came after the laymen became honest enough to confess their sins. Luke reports: "And a number of those who practiced magic arts brought their books together and burned them in the sight of all. . . . the word of the Lord grew and prevailed mightily" (Acts 19:-19,20).

If Christians were to confess their sins to God, they would experience the spiritual renewal which is desperately needed today. If Christians would seek a renewed fellowship with Christ, a multitude of unregenerated church members would begin to follow suit. Then we would begin to see people take the church seriously once again. We would see such things as those the Ephesian church witnessed. Persons would discard their astrology books for Bibles, their horoscopes for hymnbooks, and their shallow secular pursuits for the rewarding adventure of Christian discipleship. Revival would explode among us, and we would begin to see ". . . the word of the Lord [grow] and [prevail] mightily" (Acts 19:20).

But we need more than confession of sin; we also need to forsake our sin. The Bible takes a radical attitude toward sin. We tend to treat sin surprisingly lightly in view of God's intense hatred of it. God loves *sinners*, but he hates sin. The very purpose of the incarnation of Jesus Christ was to deal with our sins. ". . . you shall call his name Jesus, for he will save his people from their sins" (Matthew 1:21).

Some of the first words of Jesus' public ministry were about sin: ". . . Jesus began to preach, saying, 'Repent, for the kingdom of heaven is at hand' " (Matthew 4:17). "Repentance" is used many, many times in the Bible. The word *repentance* means basically *to change one's mind*, a reorientation of one's personality. It implies a 180 degree turn in attitude.

Repentance consists of two things: a turning *from* and a turning *to*. To repent is to turn from the old patterns and to turn to the new; to turn from sin and to turn to God. Repentance means a complete change of attitude and action.

I have a minister friend named Peter who is a former missionary. He told me that once in India he and his wife were awakened at about midnight. Two women, a young Indian woman and her mother, were both crying and insisting that Peter pray with them.

Peter responded to their request: "Of course I'll pray, but what shall I pray about?"

The mother of the girl replied, "Pray for my daughter. She's not married and she's pregnant."

Peter counseled with them about repentance and God's

forgiveness. Then he prayed with them, asking God to take this situation and work out his will in the life of the young woman.

The two women thanked Peter profusely and then walked back out into the night.

Peter told me, "I saw the young woman a few days later in the marketplace."

"How was she doing?" I asked.

Peter shifted his weight to the other foot, frowned a bit, and said: "She was continuing her former immoral way of life. It was very evident that she hadn't changed her manner of living."

"What did you do?" I asked.

"Well," Peter said, "I went over to her and jogged her memory a little. I reminded her of her visit to the parsonage a few nights earlier. I reminded her of her tears and of our prayers together. I told her that I had been praying regularly for her since she came to see me."

"What then?"

"She smiled broadly and announced: 'Oh, it's all right now, pastor. You don't have to pray anymore. You see, I discovered that I'm not pregnant after all!' "

Being sorry for the *consequences* of sin is not repentance. Neither is being afraid someone may find you out. True repentance involves *forsaking* sin. Christ wants to save us *from* our sins, not save us *in* our sins. Discussing repentance, John writes: "My children, in writing thus to you my purpose is that you should not commit sin" (1 John 2:1 NEB).

I have had a number of discussions with persons who are marginal, or nominal church members. Often someone will say, "Oh, I know I'm not right with God. I won't be a hypocrite about it. I'm a sinner and I don't try to conceal it."

Everyone admires truthfulness. Being honest is much better than donning a religious mask and pretending we're something we're not. But admitting sin is not the same thing as turning from the sin.

There is a good illustration of what I mean in the Book of Exodus. Moses was trying to persuade Pharaoh to let the Hebrews leave Egypt and return to their own land. Pharaoh was stubborn and would not let them go. The discussion between Moses and Pharaoh is revealing: ". . . Pharaoh sent, and called Moses and Aaron, and said to them, 'I have sinned this time; the LORD is in the right, and I and my people are in the wrong' " (Exodus 9:27).

In spite of Pharaoh's concession that he was sinning and that he was in the wrong, he refused to change his ways. ". . . the heart of Pharaoh was hardened, and he did not let the people of Israel go . . ." (Exodus 9:35).

Admitting sin is a virtue; but if the admission does not change one's pattern of living, he is still out of harmony with God. His sin remains. Repentance means *leaving* one's sin. This is *turning from* the old.

Repentance also involves a *turning to* the new. Repentance is complete only when one turns to God. Deciding you need more light in a room is but the first step in illuminating a room. Only after one closes the electrical circuit by flipping the switch does light flood the room. Even so, reconciliation with God is completed only after we have turned to God, the only source of forgiveness.

Many of us make the mistake of turning to *substitutes* for God instead of God himself. I did this for many months before I ever met God in a meaningful way. I turned to such things as a general determination to do better, tithing, giving more time to the church, a resolve to make better use of my time.

Of course all of these are good, so far as they go. But they don't go far enough. Regardless of how good an activity may be, anything which stops short of God himself is less than biblical repentance.

Remember the prodigal son? In disgust, he left the hogpen. But he also went back *to his father*. He might have gone to another hogpen, or a beef corral, or a sheep ranch. But reconciliation was completed only after he returned to his father. Anything less would have short-circuited his good intentions.

God calls nations as well as individuals to repentance. The Old Testament contains an invitation which God surely intends for us to take seriously today: ". . . if my people who are called by my name humble themselves, and pray and seek my face, and turn from their wicked ways, then I will hear from heaven, and will forgive their sin and heal their land" (2 Chronicles 7:14). When we become tired enough of our personal and national sins to turn to God in repentance, he promises to forgive us and to impart his healing to us.

One final word must be said about our locked closets and unavailable keys: Reconciliation with God also includes a continuing walk in renewed obedience to Christ.

A satisfying and fruitful relationship with God includes more than refraining from willful sin. It also includes a daily walk of obedience to Christ. Refraining from known sin is the negative side of Christian discipleship; walking in obedience to Christ is the positive side. *Obedience* replaces *disobedience.*

A stone never disobeys God; it is unable to do so. But neither can a stone obey God. Stones cannot, but sons can. Above all, Christian discipleship is an interpersonal relationship between the Christian and his Lord. To understand God's will with one's mind and then fail to translate it into action is unthinkable for the serious disciple of Jesus Christ.

Very early in my Christian life, I found out by trial and error that I could be truly happy only when I asked God to show me his will, and then obeyed him. I learned something else, too. I learned that the best kind of obedience is *instant* obedience. It wasn't an easy lesson to learn because procrastination is easy for me; I just naturally tend to wait until tomorrow. But when I learned to obey God *now,* I began to enjoy my relationship with him in a way I never dreamed possible. Obedience to God opens the way for one to receive God's best.

For years I have been impressed with the attitude of Samuel. As a young boy he responded to God's call with these words: "Speak, for thy servant hears" (1 Samuel 3:10). Later, in his adult life, Samuel became one of God's prophets. And Samuel's advice is still relevant for us today:

> "Has the Lord as great delight in
>   burnt offerings and sacrifices
>   as in obeying the voice of the
>   Lord?
> Behold, to obey is better than sacri-
>   fice
>   and to hearken than the fat of

rams.
For rebellion is as the sin of
divination,
and stubbornness is as iniquity
and idolatry.

1 Samuel 15:22,23

As a young Christian I discovered the Book of John. It seemed that each word was written just for me. My determination to walk in daily obedience to Christ became even greater when I read the following passage:

I am the vine, you are the branches. He who abides in me, and I in him, he it is that bears much fruit, for apart from me you can do nothing. If a man does not abide in me, he is cast forth as a branch and withers; and the branches are gathered, thrown into the fire and burned. If you abide in me, and my words abide in you, ask whatever you will, and it shall be done for you.

John 15:5–7

What further encouragement does anyone need? To maintain locked closets and to hold on to unavailable keys doesn't really make much sense, does it? Christ wants access to the deepest closet, the highest attic room and the lowest basement corner of our lives.

When we surrender the keys to him, he helps us with our housecleaning and with the rearrangement of the furniture. I'll guarantee you that your life will be better when Christ gets his way.

6

Two Ways to Walk

"... WALK NOT ACCORDING TO THE FLESH but according to the Spirit," urges Paul as he underscores his basic teaching about the life of Christian discipleship. Expanding on the two ways to walk, he writes, "To set the mind on the flesh is death, but to set the mind on the Spirit is life and peace" (Romans 8:4,6).

Elsewhere, Paul admonishes, "... walk by the Spirit, and do not gratify the desires of the flesh. For the desires of the flesh are against the Spirit, and the desires of the Spirit are against the flesh; for these are opposed to each other ..." (Galatians 5:16,17).

There are two ways to walk, and only two ways: according to the flesh or according to the Spirit. One leads to defeat; the other leads to victory. The contrast between these two ways to walk is as great as the contrast between failure and success.

Walking After The Flesh

The term *flesh* has several uses in the Bible. Often it merely refers to humanity as a whole. For example, John the Baptist uses the term in this way when he says,

> Every valley shall be filled,
> and every mountain and hill shall be

brought low,
and the crooked shall be made
        straight,
and the rough ways shall be made
        smooth;
and all flesh shall see the salvation of
        God."

                    Luke 3:5,6

Here the term *flesh* simply means *mankind.*

The Bible sometimes uses the term *flesh* to refer to our earthly life. John uses it in this sense when he writes of Christ's birth: "And the Word [Christ] became flesh and dwelt among us . . ." (John 1:14). That is, through the incarnation, Christ joined our common humanity.

At other times, the word *flesh* refers to our bodies. Paul uses it in this manner when he talks about his thorn in the flesh (2 Corinthians 12:7). Here, *flesh* means one's physical makeup.

The human body (our flesh) is neither good nor bad, although our bodies have great potential for good or for evil. They may be used in either way. The notion that the human body is evil does not belong to the Christian viewpoint. God created our bodies and he means for us to use them in his service. Paul writes, "I appeal to you . . . to present your bodies as a living sacrifice, holy and acceptable to God . . ." (Romans 12:1). In fact, God plans for our bodies to be indwelt by his Spirit. "Do you not know that your body is a temple of the Holy Spirit within you, which you have from God?" (1 Corinthians 6:19).

Thus, the distinction between walking according to the

flesh and walking according to the Spirit does not imply any inherent sinfulness in the human body. Although we must always be aware that the appetites and weaknesses of our bodies may become beachheads for sin, our *flesh* is given us for our enjoyment and for use in God's service.

In addition to its positive uses, the term *flesh* does have a negative connotation in some parts of the Bible. When used with moral overtones, *flesh* means our finite human nature, with all its limitations and potential for evil. In other words, *flesh* denotes human personality with its impotency to ward off sin. *Flesh* is that part of our personality which is vulnerable to temptation and disobedience to God.

To walk according to the flesh means to live in such a way as to be governed by one's own desires instead of by Christ. In the Bible the word *flesh* stands as a symbol of the sinful side of man's nature. That is why some translators render flesh as *lower nature*. For example: "Live your whole life in the Spirit and you will not satisfy the desires of your lower nature" (Galatians 5:16 PHILLIPS).

One can walk according to the flesh and not necessarily be guilty of outward sins. In the Book of Galatians, Paul lists what he calls the "works of the flesh." His catalog of the sins of the flesh includes both outward and inward sins. Sins such as sexual immorality and drunkenness are included along with such inward sins as jealousy and envy. Both kinds of sins are sins of the flesh.

Walking according to the flesh is the act of permitting self-interests to dominate one's life. *Flesh* is human nature as it is without God; it is man apart from the Holy Spirit. All non-Christians necessarily walk in the flesh.

In my own life, walking according to the flesh did not

include the so-called outward sins. I was proud of my morality, and for a long time I failed to see that I had any real need for God. I went to church, but church meant little to me. I was "religious," but God was not real in my life. I did not know Christ in a personal way.

Although I lived a moral life outwardly, I did not mind lying if I thought it would make me seem better than I really was. I had a secret sense of relief when a peer's work did not measure up to mine. I had very little compassion for others, and so far as I was concerned *I* was the center of the universe.

At times I was bothered by my spiritual emptiness. But I didn't know what to do about it. I remember that before I left home for my first year at college I went to a religious advisor. I asked, "How can I be better?" What I really needed was to know God personally, but I didn't know that. All I knew was that I harbored a spiritual void in my heart.

"Why, you don't need to be better," my advisor said. "You're one of the best boys in the church. You don't need to improve very much; you're fine just as you are."

"Really?"

"Sure. Just keep up the good work."

So I went off to college with a false sense of spiritual security. From time to time, I would worry about my lack of any vital contact with God. But I consoled myself by saying, "You aren't so bad, after all."

When I first met Jesus Christ I felt as if someone had turned on a light bulb in my life. I was converted by the grace of God, and I knew it. My orientation turned from myself to Christ.

Although I already lived a clean life, externally, I had a lot of inward alterations to make. My life was completely turned around. The new center of my universe was Jesus Christ; I had experienced a tremendous change.

However, even after my conversion, I sometimes walked according to the flesh. While I reoriented much of my life around Christ, I was sometimes sidetracked by religious activity and religious work. I performed some of my religious activities for myself instead of for Christ. I did part of my religious works in the way I wanted to do them instead of in Christ's way. And most significantly, I often tried to live by my own resources instead of in the power of the Spirit. To rely on self is to walk according to the flesh, and that is what I was often doing.

Much of my problem was spiritual ignorance—ignorance of how little power I had and ignorance of how much power Christ had. I had a lifetime of experience in doing things my way, depending on my own resources. But Christ was patient with me and he began to show me how self-centered I was, even in my religion. He also showed me that I could walk according to the Spirit, for whenever the Holy Spirit rebukes a Christian, he also shows him a better way. He never tears down unless he builds up. He never pulls any human props from under us unless he is there to hold us up. Christians who really believe this do not fear God's correction nor his call to deeper commitment.

When I walked after the flesh—that is, in my own way—it was not that I did not love Christ. Nor was I consciously resisting him. But much of my activity was self-centered rather than Christ-centered, strained instead of relaxed. Slowly I began to understand that the *amount* of work I did was not important. The crucial issue was the *quality* of my work and the manner in which I did it.

I began to apprehend that Christ wants to live *his* life through his disciples, instead of them trying to live *their* lives for him. I started to relax in the Holy Spirit and let him lead me and work his will in my life. Prayer took on a new meaning. I was becoming more conscious of depending on the Holy Spirit for my daily living.

I do not say that I have arrived. I haven't. But when I learned the difference between the two ways to walk, my Christian life took on an entirely new dimension. Christ was teaching me to walk according to the Spirit rather than according to the flesh. This new understanding has made an enormous difference in my life.

Walking After The Spirit

What does it mean to walk according to the Spirit? In the New Testament, every passage urging Christians to walk according to the Spirit refers to the Holy Spirit. Not man's spirit, but God's Spirit. For example, Paul wrote, ". . . walk by the Spirit . . ." (Galatians 5:16). He was obviously referring to the Holy Spirit. He also referred to the Holy Spirit when he wrote, ". . . be aglow with the Spirit"(Romans 12:11).

Walking according to the Spirit includes four areas: *surrender, fellowship, trust,* and *fruitbearing.*

1. *Surrender* To walk according to the Spirit means, first of all, that the human spirit is surrendered to God's divine Spirit. To walk according to the Spirit is to keep Christ's will foremost. A Christian disciple who walks in the Spirit has oriented his personality around Jesus Christ.

Recently, I visited a distant seminary, and went to the cafeteria for coffee. A discussion about theology was flourishing among several students, and I joined them. The talk was relaxed and lively. One student, named Lenny, began to draw personal names into the conversation. He said, "That professor is a poor teacher. His ideas are as old-fashioned as a horse and buggy."

Another student chimed in: "Yeah, I don't like his classes; they're boring. Besides, he's dogmatic and also out of touch with the twentieth century."

"That's the absolute truth," offered a third student. "He *reads* his lectures to us."

The students looked at me to get my reaction.

I was struggling with an inner conflict. My own will suggested to me: "Say something bad to underscore what these students are saying. You can twist something the professor said that would bring a lot of laughs."

But, at the same time, the Holy Spirit was prompting, "Don't say anything negative. That wouldn't be in the spirit of Christ. Turn the conversation to something constructive."

There I sat, struggling with my own will and with what I knew to be Christ's will. The students were looking at me. I offered a silent prayer that God would help me. He did. I surrendered to God's will, and he helped me come to the professor's rescue.

Every Christian finds that conflicts arise between his will and God's will. When they do, there is no question as to whose will should win. To walk in the Spirit is to surrender to Christ's will. To fail to do so is to walk in the flesh.

Surrender is the key to Christian victory. Notice Paul's use of the word *yield* in the following passage.

Do not yield your members to sin as instruments of wickedness, but yield yourselves to God as men who have been brought from death to life, and your members . . . as instruments of righteousness. . . . Do you not know that if you yield yourselves to any one as obedient slaves, you are slaves of the one whom you obey, either of sin, which leads to death, or of obedience, which leads to righteousness? . . . For just as you once yielded your members to impurity and to greater and greater iniquity, so now yield your members to righteousness for sanctification(Romans 6:13,16,19).

People often ask: "Can a Christian yield to Christ in a single act so that the surrender will be valid for all time?"

In one sense, the answer is *no.* In most of the biblical uses of the words such as *walk, yield, abide,* and *obey,* the present tense is used in the original Greek. Therefore, a good translation is usually *continue to walk; keep on yielding; consistently abide; perpetually obey.* So in this sense, the Christian's surrender to Christ must be continuing and sustained.

The Christian life is a relationship between a disciple and his Lord. By nature, a *relationship* must be dynamic and continous. Today's obedience will not suffice for tomorrow's challenge.

However, any continuing relationship must be based on a point of beginning. Sustained surrender to God always flows from a previous resolve to do so. In this sense, an act of surrender can be permanent so long as it is maintained by regular obedience.

Most Christians who are walking according to the Spirit witness to crisis times when they made deeper commitments to God. Few Christians are able to surrender on a profoundly deep level at the time of their conversion. Of course, an *attitude* of total surrender is necessary before one can be converted to Christ. But when first converted, most persons do not know very much about the demands of Christian discipleship. They have had no experience in walking closely with Christ; they have little knowledge of the deeper implications of discipleship.

When the Christian begins to follow Christ, he soon begins to learn a great deal about himself. For instance, he learns how spiritually weak he is. And as he grows in his understanding of the Christian life, he detects new areas of his life which need to be surrendered to Christ. These new insights should lead to new crises of surrender.

So when new areas of need crop up, the Christian should not despair. Rather, he should see these as part of the normal growth process of the Christian disciple. His life is characterized by an attitude of perpetual surrender. When he sees fresh possibilities for spiritual growth, the Christian who is walking in the Spirit gladly embraces them.

2. *Fellowship* A second characteristic of those who walk according to the Spirit is that they are in close fellowship with Christ. The Spirit-filled Christian lives in vital union with Christ. Before his crucifixion, Christ prayed for such a relationship: "Just as you, Father, live in me and I live in you, I am asking that they [all Christians] may live in us . . ." (John 17:20 PHILLIPS).

Union with Christ, by the way, implies that Christians will be in fellowship with each other. There is something wrong if Christians cut themselves off from fellowship with other Christians. When disharmony between Christians occurs, it is usually because Christ is not central. Other matters—such as doctrines, creeds, or denominations—have assumed a place of undue prominence.

Broken fellowship between Christians sometimes existed in the early church. Paul vigorously sought to heal such divisions among the Corinthian Christians: "God is utterly dependable, and it is he who has called you into fellowship with his Son Jesus Christ, our Lord. Now I do beg you, my brothers, by all that our Lord Jesus Christ means to you, to speak with one voice, and not allow yourselves to be split up into parties" (1 Corinthians 1:9,10 PHILLIPS). Fellowship with God —and with fellow Christians—is an important mark of walking in the Spirit.

Fellowship with God ought to be regular and steady. This is perhaps why Paul chose the term *walk* to describe the Christian life. A walk implies steady progress—not dragging behind and not galloping ahead. There may be times when the Christian will stumble; but Christ is patient and he helps his followers to their feet again.

Regular fellowship with the Holy Spirit helps one to avoid weaving from side to side spiritually. The Spirit acts as a sort of internal gyroscope to keep the Christian on an even keel. With God's help the Christian experiences an inner stability.

The church has always recognized the importance of regular fellowship with the Holy Spirit. A traditional Christian benediction reflects the ideal:

> The grace of the Lord Jesus Christ,
> and the love of God,
> and the communion of the Holy Ghost
> be with you all.

These words are taken from the closing verse of 2 Corinthians, KJV. The Greek word for *communion* is literally *fellowship*, and most contemporary translations of the Bible use the word *fellowship* in translating the passage.

Fellowship with Christ produces a growing Christlikeness. To walk in the Spirit means learning more and more about the goodness of God. The more we fellowship with him, the more we become like him. Christians who walk in the Spirit grow in their awareness of God in all of the affairs of daily life.

3. *Trust* Another mark of walking according to the Spirit is trust. I made this discovery only after a long period of time characterized by worry.

I think I was born a worrier and fretter. Even as a Christian, I have found myself at times filled with anxiety—anxiety about my career, anxiety about money, anxiety about my Christian life. Slowly, I began to see that either Christ was totally adequate or he was not adequate at all. Although one of the fruits of the Spirit is peace, there were times when I had little peace.

One of the last things Christ told his disciples before his crucifixion was, "Peace is my parting gift to you, my own peace, such as the world cannot give. Set your troubled hearts at rest, and banish your fears" (John 14:27 NEB). And one of the last things he said before his ascension was, "Peace be with you" (John 20:26).

One evening after a particularly bad week of fretting about a minor problem, I was having dinner with a lovely Christian couple. I was not yet married, and I looked forward to any home-cooked meal. My expectations were not in vain. Sheila had prepared a delicious dinner, and the entire evening was a tonic for my turbulent spirit.

I admired the poise of this beautiful couple, and I thought to myself, "Why can't I have the trust in God that they have?" I wondered how they managed to maintain such a quiet joy. My eyes fell on a wall plaque over the buffet in the dining room. The verse on the plaque was from Isaiah: "Thou wilt keep him in perfect peace, whose mind is stayed on thee" (Isaiah 26:3 KJV).

A thought pierced my consciousness with a sharp impact: "Why, your mind isn't focused on God nearly as much as it is focused on your problems. That's why you have times of fretting and worrying."

As I sat there over a second cup of coffee, enjoying the conversation, I inwardly began to surrender to God my tendency to fret and worry. I knew I had not been trusting God as I should, and I confessed to God that I was powerless to change myself.

That brief and silent prayer marked a new beginning for me. Romans 8:28 began to become a part of my daily attitudes: ". . . everything that happens fits into a pattern for good" (PHILLIPS).

After this, I started to walk with a more conscious trust in Christ to work out the daily details in my life. The following verse took on new meaning: ". . . to set the mind on the Spirit is life and peace" (Romans 8:6). Whenever I fail to walk in the Spirit, I begin to fray around the edges. But as I daily receive the Spirit's help, I find that my natural tendency to fret is replaced by God's peace.

As a Christian worker, I have been helped in many ways as I have depended more fully on God. God is helping me with my proneness to become angry or resentful when I see a poor example of Christian behavior from a carnal "Christian." I tend to tighten up inside whenever I hear an atrocious sermon which distorts Christian truth. Part of me wants to react as if the Kingdom of God depends on how well I defend the gospel.

But the Kingdom of God belongs to *him,* not me. And his kingdom will survive bad sermons and un-Christian "Christians." Christ said, ". . . I will build my church; the powers of Hades shall not succeed against it" (Matthew 16:18 MOFFATT).

Another lesson I've learned is that Christ will always bless his word. Sometimes God works in unpredictable ways. Sometimes like yeast. Sometimes like the mighty wind. But he promises to use a faithful witness to his gospel. As long as I witness to *Christ,* I can trust God that my witness will accomplish something good.

Christ has not called his disciples to be his warriors; he has called them to be his witnesses. This fact means that the Christian does not have to concern himself about judging others or with "putting them in their places." Such activity betrays a lack of trust that the Holy Spirit is at work and that Christ truly is building his church.

God invites the Christian to a life of quiet trust. And trust in God is a mark of walking in the Spirit. Trust cannot be mustered up from within, but it can be received from Christ as a gift.

Surrender to Christ, *fellowship* with Christ, and *trust* in Christ will lead to *fruit.*

4. *Fruit* A final mark of the Christian disciple who walks according to the Spirit is fruit. Christ did not say that Christians *might* bear fruit, or that Christians *should* bear fruit. He promised that Christians *would* bear fruit.

Christ did, however, give a condition for fruit-bearing.

That condition is that we live in close communion with him. In other words, we are to walk in the Spirit. Jesus said, "He who dwells in me, as I dwell in him, bears much fruit; for apart from me you can do nothing" (John 15:5 NEB). Christians are not called to be museum pieces for display; they are called to bear fruit. ". . . I chose you and appointed you," Jesus said, "that you should go and bear fruit and that your fruit should abide . . ." (John 15:16).

Precisely what is *fruit?* For some time, I struggled with this question. I knew I was supposed to bear fruit, but I wasn't quite sure what fruit was.

I had known Christ for only about three weeks when a friend asked me to go with him to hear a speaker in a nearby church. My friend said that the minister was a famous evangelist. I had never heard of this person, but I went along with my friend.

In the sermon, the evangelist insisted, "There's only one kind of fruit in the Christian life."

I sat bolt upright in the pew, listening intently.

He continued. "That fruit is soul winning—yes sir, soul winning!"

I wilted because I was not a soul winner.

Then the speaker went on to expound the virtues of leading others to Christ. He made it clear that soul winning was the greatest, if not the only, virtue in the Christian life. "Fruit-bearing is soul winning," he declared.

As a new Christian, I didn't question what he said, for I thought that everything a minister said about religion was probably true. Yet I knew I had not won anyone for Christ. In fact, the people with whom I had shared my new faith were not very interested at all. And according to the sermon

I was hearing, the only fruit worthy of mention was soul winning. I thought, "I'm not a soul winner. In fact, I seem to scare souls away. I'm not bearing fruit at all."

Worried about my lack of "fruit," I began to search the Bible. In the Book of Galatians I read for the first time about the works of the flesh and the fruit of the Spirit. ". . . the fruit of the Spirit is love, joy, peace, patience, kindness, goodness, faithfulness, gentleness, self-control . . ." (Galatians 5:22,23).

Was I relieved! Here I saw that fruit was much more than soul winning. In fact, soul winning was not even mentioned in the chapter.

Over the next several months, two conclusions emerged. First, I concluded that the fruits of the Spirit are primarily *moral virtues.* That is, they have to do with the relationships and the character of the Christian. I saw that fruit is more than activity for God; it is a quality of existence before God. The list in Galatians provides a perfect blend of being and doing.

Second, I saw that the fruit of the Spirit is exactly that— it is the fruit of the *Holy Spirit.* Not my fruit, but the Spirit's fruit. I noticed the contrast between the *works* of the flesh and the *fruit* of the Spirit. Works suggest struggle and effort. Fruit suggests a branch which partakes of the energy and life of the vine. Christian fruit is a natural result of walking in the Spirit.

I saw that Christian fruit never depended on how hard I worked for Christ, but on how completely I trusted Christ and depended on *his working in me!* My task is to abide; the Spirit's work is to bear the fruit. Christian fruit is the harvest of the Holy Spirit.

The promise of God to those who follow him in loving

discipleship is that they will bear fruit. Jesus said, ". . . you will know them by their fruits" (Matthew 7:20).

The New Testament teaches that regenerated Christians have received the Holy Spirit and therefore that they should let the Spirit control their lives. "If the Spirit is the source of our life, let the Spirit also direct our course" (Galatians 5:25 NEB). The Spirit who brings the Christian into new life also provides the dynamic to live that life.

Thus, there are two ways to walk: after the flesh or after the Spirit. In the flesh we cannot succeed; in the Spirit we cannot fail. ". . . our lower nature has no claim upon us; we are not obliged to live on that level. If you do so, you must die. But if by the Spirit you put to death all the base pursuits of the body, then you will live" (Romans 8:12,13 NEB).

7
Accepting the Dawn

AN ANCIENT WISE MAN who loved God once wrote, ". . . the path of the righteous is like the light of dawn, which shines brighter and brighter until full day" (Proverbs 4:18). This beautiful sentence serves as an apt description of the life of the Christian disciple.

The Christian life is frequently characterized by *light:* ". . . the people who sat in darkness have seen a great light, and for those who sat in the region and shadow of death light has dawned" (Matthew 4:16). The Apostle John wrote to an early Christian congregation, reminding them, ". . . the darkness is passing away and the true light is already shining" (1 John 2:8). Pursuing the same thought, Paul announced to the Christians of his time, ". . . you are all sons of light and sons of the day . . ." (1 Thessalonians 5:5).

One enters into a life of Christian discipleship by accepting Jesus Christ who is the light of the world. When the light of Christ dawns in the heart, one experiences supernatural change within. John wrote that Christ is the "true light," and to those who receive him in their hearts is granted the privilege of becoming "children of God" (John 1:9–13). Christians have received in their hearts a new dawn—the dawning of the light of Jesus Christ. They have experienced the new birth, without which Jesus declared one "cannot see the kingdom of God" (John 3:3).

When I discovered this light, I entered for the first time into a personal relationship with Christ. Immediately, I wanted to learn more about the Christian life. Hungrily, I listened to sermons and devoured religious books. But I soon began to be troubled about something.

I noticed that most of the sermons I heard fell into either of two categories: the type of sermon which *never* mentioned the possibility of the new birth or the type of sermon which dealt with almost nothing *but* the new birth.

Sermons of the first variety were vague; they seemed to equate morality or social action with Christian faith. I knew from personal experience that morality and doing good were a long way from vital religion.

Sermons of the second variety seemed to me to repeat the same theme over and over: "You must be born again." Listening to these sermons, I wondered if there was anything else to the Christian faith other than being born again.

I got a measure of help from these sermons, but many of them were not meeting my spiritual needs. At first, I thought that something was wrong with me, and I wondered if my commitment to Christ had faltered. I felt guilty because I wasn't getting very much from many of the sermons I heard. Although the sermons contained truth, they were not helping me to grow spiritually.

Occasionally, I heard an excellent sermon on Christian maturity. Or a sermon on how to apply my Christian faith to daily life. Such sermons helped me very much, and they encouraged me greatly. But I sensed that I needed more.

One day I read a Scripture passage which immediately

seized my attention: ". . . let us leave the elementary doctrines of Christ and go on to maturity, not laying again a
foundation of repentance from dead works and of faith toward God . . ." (Hebrews 6:1). The passage set me to thinking.
I checked the Phillips translation and found this rendering:
"Let us leave behind the elementary teaching about Christ
and go forward to adult understanding. Let us not lay over
and over again the foundation truths—repentance from the
deeds which led to death, believing in God. . . ."

What this said to me was: "The elementary doctrines of the
Christian faith are that you must turn from your own works
which lead to death, and turn in repentance to Jesus Christ
for your salvation. But don't spend all your time on elementary teachings. Start your adventure into Christian maturity.
Go beyond foundational truths and move toward a more
adult understanding of your life in Christ."

I developed the conviction that the Christian life is a *con-
tinuous dawn!* Christ never ceases to shed new light upon
the human heart. Christian conversion is only the beginning
of a life of exciting spiritual adventure. Once the light of
Christ dawns in the human personality, the dawn leads to a
greater and greater apprehension of light. I began to see that
when I became a Christian I had just been *introduced* to
light; there was an infinite amount of dawn yet to accept.

In one way, to know Christ is to have everything; but in
another way, conversion launches one out as a new pilgrim
on an endless journey. I think of it this way: When an acorn
sprouts, it is a complete oak tree. But in another way, it is
only the beginning of the oak. The young oak has as much life
as it ever will have, but it lacks maturity.

In the same way, Christian disciples need to spend an

entire lifetime maturing in Christ. Peter gave sound advice to the maturing Christian: "... grow in the grace and knowledge of our Lord and Savior Jesus Christ" (2 Peter 3:18).

What had been bothering me was that most of the sermons that I heard seldom went beyond the elementary teaching of the gospel. It was not that I disagreed with what I heard preached. It was just that I longed for more depth. My feelings of frustration could be expressed in this way: "Okay, I *know* that I must be born again. I agree that you must repent. So, I've repented. So what now?" I needed instruction on how to mature in my discipleship. I did not particularly need to hear repeatedly, "You must be born again."

As I look back on my experience, I see now that the Holy Spirit was teaching me that Christ offers a perpetually new dawn. He calls his disciples to greater maturity because he loves them and because he wants to share his life with them by helping them to become everything they are capable of becoming. Christ awakens the Christian out of drowsiness to face a new dawn, not to make him unhappy, but in order to invite him to a new and exciting future.

Paul wrote with satisfaction to a congregation of young Christians: "We are bound to give thanks to God always for you, brethren, as is fitting, because your faith is growing abundantly . . ." (2 Thessalonians 1:3). To another group of believers he wrote that his purpose as a minister was to lead each one of them to "full maturity in Christ Jesus" (Colossians 1:28 PHILLIPS).

The phrase *new birth* never appears in Paul's writings. The absence of the phrase does not mean that Paul disregarded Christian conversions or that he felt it unimportant. Rather, Paul's readers had already experienced spiritual regeneration, and he was determined to lead them into Christian maturity.

Paul himself was constantly moving ahead in his Christian experience. In a revealing personal witness, he wrote, ". . . I do not consider myself to have 'arrived,' spiritually, nor do I consider myself already perfect. But I keep going on, grasping ever more firmly that purpose for which Christ Jesus grasped me. My brothers, I do not consider myself to have fully grasped it even now. But . . . I go straight for the goal . . ." (Philippians 3:12–14 PHILLIPS). Here was a growing man, a maturing man—a man who was constantly accepting the dawn.

Why are we so slow to move ahead toward Christian maturity? One reason is that many of us are not aware that our Christian life can rise above the humdrum of daily sameness. We tend to accept mediocrity as normal.

I spoke recently at a union meeting of six denominations in a western city. A few days before I was scheduled to begin speaking, a large number of lay witnesses from several states came to the city. These laymen were from a number of denominations, including United Methodist, Presbyterian, Baptist, and Roman Catholic. The lay witnesses were all exceptionally vital Christians, and their lives made a profound impression on the church members of that city.

After I arrived, I heard three different laymen make the following statements:

—"I didn't know Christians like that even existed except in fiction."

—"Those lay witnesses inspired me to begin a new quest for Christian maturity."

—"The idea of knowing God like that was completely foreign to me."

The lay witnesses had brought a new vision and a new hope to many of the church members of that city. By the time I arrived, the entire town pulsed with religious excitement. Many persons, for the first time, had become aware that Christian discipleship could be more than a dull routine.

Part of our failure to mature as Christ's disciples is due to a low expectation of the Christian life. Many of us have a limited vision and a weak motivation. Often, we have seen so much anemic Christianity that we fail to realize that virile Christianity is even a possibility. Many Christians do not expect their Christian life to be exciting. And it isn't.

Before a Christian can be renewed, he must receive a new vision of what God promises to do for his people. Christians need to see the possibilities of a new dawn before they can experience the renewal so badly needed in the church. "Where there is no vision, the people perish (Proverbs 29:18 KJV). An encouraging sign today is that many Christians are asking God to renew their spiritual vision and make them agents of enthusiasm.

Another reason Christians do not mature as they should is because of fear. All of us at times have a fear of what God might ask us to do. We tend to cling to the comfort of the status quo. Often, the good gets in the way of what is better. Sometimes the preoccupation with past blessings prevents present advances.

I know a rural congregation of Christians in the East that for years was satisfied with its comfortable routine. The church schedule was convenient, and it met the needs of the congregation. However, the church had almost no outreach into the community.

A denominational official proposed a merger of the congregation with a congregation formerly of another denomination. Merger had already been consummated on the denominational level, but the congregation resisted a local merger. The people complained that they did not know the people in the other congregation. "And besides," said the chairman of the church board, "we have been in competition with the other congregation for over one hundred years."

One member revealed the real reason for their reluctance to merge: "We just don't want to lose what we already have. We're comfortable, and we're afraid of anything that might upset our nice church."

However, through a series of circumstances, the congregations did merge. And how glad they were that they did! Merger was hard work, certainly, but the results were spectacular. New friendships developed; each congregation strengthened the other. The "marriage" worked, and in a short time they were one in spirit. As a result of the merger the new congregation began to extend its ministry into the community. New persons are now coming to church, and the congregation is experiencing spiritual renewal.

By no means will church mergers solve all church problems, nor will they necessarily bring spiritual renewal. But merger was what *these* congregations needed. The point is that a new opportunity was bidding, but *fear* threatened to block significant advancement. These Christians overcame their inertia and a new day dawned for the united congregation.

We tend to want to be in control of everything. We feel most comfortable when we can predict the directions our lives will take. We like to keep our religion in neat packages and tidy boxes, and we fear the unpredictable or anything that we cannot manipulate. Sometimes we even want to control God's actions in our lives because any uncertainty poses a threat to us.

But Christ refuses to be contained in a straightjacket. His Spirit is never subject to our whims or desires. Jesus compared the Holy Spirit to the wind: "The wind blows where it wills, and you hear the sound of it, but you do not know whence it comes or whither it goes..." (John 3:8). He likened the gospel to wine which cannot be contained in unsuitable wineskins.

Unless we become willing for Christ to upset our plans and programs, he cannot accomplish his will in us. Either we are in control of our lives or Christ is.

Often we forget that Christ's plans for us are much superior to anything we could concoct ourselves. He does not call us to the routine and the normal, nor always to the safe and the predictable. But he does call us to a life greater than anything we can dream of. He beckons us to a spiritual adventure that will affect all that we do in daily life. He summons us into a new dawn.

Recently, on a trip, my wife and I stopped at a motel for the evening. One of our boys—the nine year old—was with us. I suggested that he go swimming in the pool.

Once in the pool, I urged him to learn to dive. He began to hedge because he was afraid. He said, "Dad, swimming's fine; but I don't want to go off the deep end."

I kept encouraging him. Four adults who were sitting at an

outdoor table nearby heard me coaxing Kenny to dive. They became interested, and gradually they formed a miniature cheering section. They shouted to my son, "Come on, Kenny; we know you can do it!"

Finally, Kenny got up the courage to walk out on the diving board. He looked down into the water, and his eyes opened so wide that he appeared to be staring down into an active volcano. As he stood there thinking it over, the cheering section started in again: "Come on, Kenny, we know you can do it!"

Kenny had gone too far to turn back now. So he took a deep breath and bravely plunged in head first. He surfaced and paddled to the side, amidst the applause of his well-wishers. He dived again and again. Some of his efforts were real belly whoppers, but Kenny learned to dive. His cheering section remained exuberant. Kenny was enjoying himself so much we could hardly get him out of the pool to shower for dinner.

An hour later during our meal in the motel dining room, Kenny spied his cheering section having dinner across the room. He waved to them and turned to me and said softly, "Dad, thanks a lot for helping me learn to dive." What he had once resisted was now one of his greatest delights.

Like Kenny, we are all sometimes reluctant to respond to fresh challenges—we seem slow to accept God's invitation to new adventures. Yet, after we do "dive in" we wonder why we took so long to respond.

Another reason we fail to mature spiritually is because we suffer from discouragement. From time to time we are tempted to lose heart because of some difficulty we encounter. Even New Testament Christians sometimes lost the sparkle from their Christian experience. ". . . let us not grow weary in well-doing," wrote Paul, "for in due season we shall reap, if we do not lose heart" (Galatians 6:9).

We lose heart when we fail to keep our eyes on Jesus. This happened to Peter. Once, Jesus came to his disciples in a boat, walking on the sea. Peter recognized Jesus, and Jesus invited Peter to come to him.

Peter immediately stepped over the side of the boat. He did fine for awhile: as long as he looked at Jesus, he walked on the water. But when Peter's eyes strayed from the Lord and when he looked at his own circumstances, he began to sink.

Christians can do anything Christ invites them to do so long as they keep their eyes on him. But when they begin to rely upon their own resources and gaze at the difficult circumstances around them, they start to "sink." The only way any Christian can avoid discouragement is to keep his attention fixed on Christ, and as he does so, Christ imparts his adequacy.

Perhaps one of the main reasons we get our eyes off Christ is that we are preoccupied with material things. Materially, our lives are more complicated than at any other time since man's creation.

Jesus spoke directly to this issue in a parable. He told of a farmer who planted seeds in a field. The seeds sprouted and showed promise of bearing a good harvest. However, thistles also sprouted in the field and they choked out the good seed.

Commenting on the story, Jesus said, "That [seed] which fell among thistles represents those who hear, but their further growth is choked by cares and wealth and pleasures of life, and they bring nothing to maturity" (Luke 8:14 NEB).

It is never easy to keep material things in proper perspective. The need for a Christian attitude toward money and possessions has become one of our greatest challenges today. Our contemporary life requires that we become deeply involved with gadgets, large and small. We cannot avoid being a part of a technological society, a society that demands a deep involvement with material things. Of course it is neither possible nor desirable to extract one's self from our modern world. We need not sell everything we have and join a monastery in order to avoid the dangers of materialism. The answer to the threat of secularism lies in keeping material matters in a secondary place and giving absolute priority to Jesus Christ. Such a relationship with Christ can be accomplished only by daily surrender to his lordship.

Pride remains as another reason we fail to grow to Christian maturity. If we ever become satisfied with our spirituality, Christ can do little for us. Our tendency to overlook our spiritual needs is one reason John wrote, "If we say we have no sin, we deceive ourselves, and the truth is not in us. If we confess our sins, he is faithful and just, and will forgive our sins and cleanse us from all unrighteousness. If we say we have not sinned, we make [God] a liar, and his word is not in us" (1 John 1:8-10).

We dare not let pride keep us from God's forgiving and renewing grace. Pride was the downfall of the Pharisees. Their spiritual smugness blocked their ability to see that they had any spiritual needs.

The maturing Christian carefully guards against spiritual pride. He knows that in himself he has no ability to overcome sin. The longer he walks with Christ the more he discovers his own limitations. He confesses with Paul, ". . . I can will what is right, but I cannot do it" (Romans 7:18). The Christian's entire spiritual life depends on God's grace and God's power.

We do not have to look very hard to find reasons to postpone accepting the dawn of new spiritual adventure. Excuses, guises, pretenses, explanations, and bluffs are easy to come by. I know, because I have come up with some fine ones myself! But I have found that my greatest advances in Christian discipleship have been made when I surrendered my fear, hesitation and excuse-making to Christ.

The growth to which Christ calls each Christian beckons as his highest fulfillment and his greatest privilege. The options before every Christian are to stumble around in semidarkness or eagerly to accept the dawn into which Christ continually calls.

Christian growth is never automatic. It does not come about spontaneously any more than logs float upstream. Nor does growth come merely by *wishing*. Far from being involuntary, Christian growth hinges on several conditions.

Christians must have certain specific attitudes if they are to avoid settling down into a dull and ineffective Christian existence. These attitudes do not result from accident, nor are they the product of our genes.

However, with God's help, you can *will* to have the necessary attitudes. If you do not have the proper orientation for Christian growth and maturity, ask God to make you *willing to be willing.*

These four attitudes are basic to accepting the dawn of a greater apprehension of God: (1) honesty, (2) humility, (3) sensitivity and (4) hunger.

1. *Honesty*   Many centuries ago, Jeremiah, an Old Testa-

ment prophet, wrote one of the most penetrating statements about man that has ever been penned. He wrote, "The heart is deceitful above all things, and desperately corrupt; who can understand it?" (Jeremiah 17:9). Man tries to fool others and he tries to fool himself. Deception is man's natural way, and it stems from a basic lack of honesty.

Most of us find it fairly easy to be honest about others, but we find it very difficult to be honest about ourselves. Jesus said that we can see a speck in our neighbor's eye, but we fail to see an entire log in our own eye.

The Christian who is intent on serious spiritual growth must, above all, be honest. Absolute transparency in God's presence is fundamental to any spiritual advancement. We do not enjoy taking a completely impartial look at ourselves because we do not like what we see. In fact, without God's help we cannot be really honest about our spiritual shortcomings. The psalm writer knew this, and he prayed, "Search me, O God, and know my heart! Try me and know my thoughts! And see if there be any wicked way in me, and lead me in the way everlasting!" (Psalms 139:23,24).

You may not use those exact words, but the spirit of that ancient prayer is essential if one is to be open and honest before God. When anyone begins to exercise genuine honesty, God will begin to show him areas of spiritual need.

Jesus was unable to help many of the religious leaders in the New Testament because of their lack of honesty. They saw the spiritual needs of others around them, but they failed to see the needs of their own hearts.

Jesus illustrated man's lack of honesty with a story in which he told about two men who went to the house of prayer. One man said, "God, I thank thee that I am not like other men . . . ." Then he proceeded to give God a long catalog of his own virtues. By way of contrast, the other man felt a sense of unworthiness before God. In deep sorrow, he said, "God, be merciful to me a sinner!" (Luke 18:11,13).

One man lacked the honesty to see his great sin of pride. The other man had the openness to admit and confess his sin. Jesus left no doubt as to which man received God's forgiveness.

As we spend more time talking to God in prayer, we find it easier to be honest with ourselves and with God. Our own concerns and our preoccupation with ourselves can become great hindrances to honesty. Taking more time in God's presence will lead us to see ourselves better; we can also apprehend more clearly the resources of God's grace.

2. *Humility*   One of the paradoxes of the Christian faith: The way up is always down. Peter put it quite directly: "God opposes the proud, but gives grace to the humble" (1 Peter 5:5). And Jesus taught, "Whoever humbles himself like [a] child, he is the greatest in the kingdom of heaven" (Matthew 18:4). Humility is willingness to take second place.

A beautiful example of a humble spirit is John the Baptist. As a young minister, John became enormously popular. People from far and wide came to hear his sermons, and even the religious leaders were impressed by his mighty ministry. His success, however, did not delude him into trusting in his own abilities. The secret of his amazing success and power came from his humble spirit.

On one occasion, the leaders of the Jewish religious world approached John and asked him, "Who are you?" This question was their way of saying, "We recognize that you are a unique spiritual leader. Are you God's prophet? Someone special? Tell us, John, who are you, anyway?" Unassumingly, John confessed that he was only a lesser light, and that Christ was the true light.

The humility demanded of the Christian disciple is so radical that the New Testament compares it to *death*. And the metaphor of death best describes the Christian's attitude toward his own desires, rights, and prerogatives. Paul uses this term many times. For example: ". . . put yourselves at the disposal of God, as dead men raised to life; yield your bodies to him as implements for doing right . . ." (Romans 6:13 NEB).

Jesus declared, "Truly, truly I say to you, unless a grain of wheat falls into the earth and dies, it remains alone; but if it dies, it bears much fruit. He who loves his life loses it, and he who hates his life in this world will keep it for eternal life" (John 12:24,25). As one dies to personal plans and aims, God exalts him, uses him, and enormously multiples his abilities.

Perhaps one of our greatest mistakes consists of assuming that a commitment made to God sometime in the past remains perpetually valid. Rather, Christian discipleship flourishes as a one-to-one relationship with God sustained on a daily basis. A Christian dentist said to me, "I asked Christ to nail me to his cross, but later I climbed down again and went about my own business." How typical of many of us!

I once began to worry about an unresolved situation in my work which I had earlier committed to God. My wife said to me, "I thought you surrendered that problem to God over a month ago."

Sheepishly, I replied, "I did."

She responded, "Well, if you surrendered it to God, what are you trying to do, 'unsurrender it'?"

I saw her point, and I recommitted the situation to God

once more and determined no longer to worry about the situation. In due time, God worked the matter out in a beautiful way, all without my fretting and stewing!

As a Christian walks with Christ, he continually gains new insights into the amazing splendor of God and his ways. No one could possibly comprehend the multitude of Christ's mysteries all at one time. But Christ unfolds them to his disciples as they mature and as they are able to grasp them. The grace and glory of Christ can be apprehended only by a humble attitude. There is no other way to grow spiritually. Humility realizes that it can quickly become blatant pride without God's continual help. Humility does not try to justify itself; it accepts the reality of its own limitations, and eagerly opens itself to God's divine working.

3. *Sensitivity*   Only the spiritually sensitive person can receive anything from God. One's spiritual radar must be tuned in to God, because without openness to him Christian growth is impossible.

Jesus told the apostles not to ". . . throw your pearls before swine . . ." (Matthew 7:6). He seems to be saying, "You're wasting your time trying to minister to individuals who have no sensitivity to spiritual matters. Leave such persons alone until they are prepared to listen to spiritual truth." The reason Jesus remained silent at his trial before Pilate was that Pilate was insensitive to spiritual values and to any words Jesus might have uttered.

The importance of spiritual sensitivity is emphasized again and again by Jesus. Think, for example, of his parable of the four types of soil, sometimes called the Parable of the Sower (Matthew 13:3-23). All four types of soil represent different attitudes of the human heart.

One type of soil Jesus called ground by the wayside. Jesus was saying that some people's hearts are like ground packed as hard as a pathway pounded by the footprints of generations of travellers. Even as the farmer's seed cannot penetrate such inhospitable soil, so the word of God cannot break through an insensitive attitude. The gist of what Jesus was saying is, "Unless you become responsive to spiritual matters, the word of God cannot germinate in your heart and produce a bountiful harvest."

Some may say, "Of course, I agree that right religion demands spiritual sensitivity. But sensitivity to what?" The New Testament answer is "Sensitivity to the Holy Spirit as he makes Jesus Christ more real to us."

One of the important ways the Holy Spirit speaks to contemporary man is through the Bible. Little wonder the Bible continues to dominate as a best seller. Christians find it indispensable to their spiritual growth. Through the witness of the Bible, we begin to see Christ more clearly. And Christ is the summation of God's revelation to men.

To be sure, God has spoken to the human family in various ways. For example, he once spoke through prophets of the Old Testament, and even now he continues to speak through circumstances and through the conscience of man. But, more clearly, he communicates to us through Jesus Christ. A first-century disciple wrote, "God, who gave to our forefathers many different glimpses of the truth in the words of the prophets, has now, at the end of the present age, given us the truth in the Son" (Hebrews 1:1,2 PHILLIPS).

Jesus Christ is the *supreme* and *final* revelation of God. The Bible reliably points us to Christ. As we listen to the message of the Bible, the Holy Spirit begins to speak to us in ways impossible to misunderstand. Of course, the Bible is not a *magic* book, but it is a *miraculous* book—a unique book, quite superior to any other.

Someone may say, "I want to be sensitive to God; but I just don't seem to *feel* anything." Every Christian has experienced such a concern. I, too, have experienced times when I had no religious feeling, times when I had little emotional desire to obey God. I find persons in the Bible who also had times when they had to walk by raw faith, with little help from their emotions.

The Psalms contain classic illustrations of walking by faith and not by sight. Even David, who was "a man after God's own heart," sometimes lacked any exuberant religious feelings:

> How long, O LORD? Wilt thou
>   forget me for ever?
> How long wilt thou hide thy face
>   from me?
> How long must I bear pain in my
>   soul,
>   and have sorrow in my heart all
>   the day?
>
> Psalms 13:1,2

Here was a man who experienced the depths of emotional despair.

Or consider John the Baptist: He languished in a dreary Roman jail for a long period of time. Such confinement was difficult for an activist like John. His lack of religious emotion erupted into periods of doubt. Finally, he sent a message to

Jesus: "Are you he who is to come, or shall we look for another?" (Matthew 11:3). He tottered on the verge of doubting Christ himself.

Then there was Paul: Being human, he often suffered times when his religious feelings ran almost dry. Yet, through faith he was able to live above the capricious tricks of his emotions. Once he wrote, "We are afflicted in every way, but not crushed; perplexed, but not driven to despair; persecuted, but not forsaken; struck down, but not destroyed . . ." (2 Corinthians 4:8,9). He found through experience that Christians have to walk, at times, with nothing to sustain them but trust in God.

As we grow in Christ, he weans us from dependence upon feelings, which are based in ourselves, and points us to faith, which is based in God. As the Christian exercises faith, feeling and emotion spring to life in due time. Faith leads the train of our religious experience down the track; often our emotions must come along on the caboose.

Emotions are never dependable enough to build one's faith upon because we cannot will the direction of our feelings. We can, however, will the direction of our faith. And in time faith primes the pump of our emotions. Thus, the maturing Christian never allows his emotions to determine his Christian commitment. He learns to remain sensitive to the Holy Spirit even if his emotions threaten to sidetrack him from trust in God.

4. *Hunger* A final requirement for Christian growth is spiritual hunger. Spiritual growth and maturity depend upon desiring God more than anything else in the world. Jesus announced, "Blessed are those who hunger and thirst for righteousness, for they shall be satisfied" (Matthew 5:6).

Paul had an enormous spiritual appetite, and he refused ever to become content with past experiences. His attitude shines forth through these words: ". . . forgetting what lies behind and straining forward to what lies ahead, I press on toward the goal for the prize of the upward call of God in Christ Jesus" (Phillippians 3:13,14).

An appetite for God never originates in man. Rather, a hunger for God results from a *prior* work of God's grace in man's heart. Jesus said, "Nobody comes to me unless he is drawn to me by the Father who sent me . . ." (John 6:44 PHILLIPS). Through the Holy Spirit God calls us to himself. John records God's invitation: "Come forward, you who are thirsty; accept the water of life, a free gift to all who desire it" (Revelation 22:17 NEB). Man's response is always preceded by God's call.

If a person does not feel hunger for Christian growth, it is not because God has neglected him; it is because he has neglected God. Many Christians unfortunately have not yet apprehended that "You do not have, because you do not ask" (James 4:2). Christ encourages his followers to ask big things of God. We have his promise: "Ask and you shall receive" (*see* John 15:7). God's working in our lives is often hindered by our lack of desire.

Ceaselessly, Christ calls his disciples to an ever-expanding future—a future characterized by maturity, creativity, and excellence. But most of all, it is a future of *light*. "While you have the light, believe in the light, that you may become sons of light" (John 12:36).

Christian, your path can become like the light of dawn, a dawn which shines brighter and brighter until the full day when you shall be with Christ. Until that time comes, accept the dawn of new opportunity which he offers. In doing so you can reach your full potential as a human being and as a Christian disciple.

8
Putting on the Yoke

A SWIMMER is never a true swimmer until he plunges into the water. A baker is not a true baker until he gets out his pans and begins to knead the bread dough with his hands. A college student is not fully a student until he opens his books and experiences the thrill and excitement of new discovery. A hunting dog it not a true hunting dog until he bounds out into an open field and works harmoniously with his master.

Similarly, a Christian is not a true disciple until he puts on the yoke of Christ and begins to walk in obedient fellowship with his Master. Jesus' invitation is, "Come to me, all who labor and are heavy laden, and I will give you rest. Take my yoke upon you, and learn from me . . . and you will find rest for your souls. For my yoke is easy, and my burden is light" (Matthew 11:28-30).

Unfortunately, numerous church members have never really taken Christ's yoke upon themselves. They are like swimmers who only look at the water, bakers who are content to memorize recipes, students who merely sharpen pencils, hunting dogs who bark but do not run. As a result of their partial involvement in Christian discipleship they fail to experience the full life which Christ intends for them.

But there is a better way. The better way is putting on Christ's yoke; it is an all-out commitment to discipleship.

"Taking Christ's yoke" means full submission to Christ and following him in radical obedience.

In the passage just quoted, Christ gives two invitations: (1) *Come to me* and (2) *Take my yoke upon you.* The first invitation, *come to me,* speaks of a commitment which results in new spiritual life. The second invitation, *take my yoke upon you,* implies an obedience which leads to complete fulfillment.

Some Christians emphasize the *foundation* of the Christian life, conversion. Other Christians emphasize the *superstructure* of the Christian life, service. Unfortunately, many of us tend to respond only to *part* of Christ's invitation. The result is that we have often separated what Christ intended as a whole; thus our Christianity becomes either sterile or without lasting results. Christ's invitation is both to come to him (conversion) and to take up his yoke (service). For the Christian, Jesus is both Saviour and Lord. Both parts of his invitation must be given due attention by the serious disciple.

Many would-be disciples, however, find it easier to come to Christ for pardon than to follow him in obedience. For these persons full surrender seems difficult. A college student said to me, "I'm afraid of God; I'm afraid that his plans for me will make me very unhappy."

I assured her that God never makes our lives unpleasant. Rather, he wants to give us joy. Christ said, "My yoke is easy." The word *easy* in the original text means "useful" or "good." The New English Bible translates the passage, ". . . my yoke is good to bear. . . ." Jesus is saying, "The life I have planned for you fits you perfectly, and it is designed for your greatest good and happiness."

But you may ask, "How can I really be sure that I can trust God? A young physician put it like this: "How can I know that God won't make a mess of my life if I take his way?" A middle-aged businessman used these words, "How can I be sure God will catch me if I take a 'leap of faith' toward him?"

There is only one answer to these questions: Our basis of belief rests on what Jesus has said. We can believe the Christian message because Jesus gave it. His person stands behind his word, and his word is the final basis of our faith.

In Paul's day, people were no different than they are today. Paul wrote: ". . . Jews demand signs [miracles] and Greeks seek wisdom" (1 Corinthians 1:22). That is, the Jewish people demanded that Christ astound them with his spectacular miracles and wonders. On the other hand, the Gentiles insisted on receiving a sophisticated intellectual system—something "rational" that was couched in philosophical words and phrases.

Christ had faced similar demands for proof of what he was saying. Luke reports Jesus as saying, "This generation is an evil generation; it seeks a sign . . ." (Luke 11:29). Jesus went on to say that the only sign that he would give was *himself.* Jesus does not give signs—*he is the sign.*

After I became a Christian, I saw that man's prerogative is not to decide whether Christ's sayings are true. That is a decision which no one is really at liberty to make. The only choice any of us has is: "Do I accept his word or don't I?" The Christian lives by faith in Christ's words, not by signs or proofs.

Contemporary demands for scientific proof or philosophical proof for the validity of the gospel are not unlike similar clamors found in the New Testament. On one occasion Jesus' listeners said, "Then what sign do you do, that we may see, and believe you?" (John 6:30). They went on to recall how Moses gave their ancestors a miraculous sign of bread in the desert.

But Jesus simply retorted, "I am the bread of life; he who comes to me shall not hunger, and he who believes in me shall never thirst" (John 6:35). Jesus' point was that we must believe him simply on the basis of his word. He does not cater to our desires by conjuring up bread; he is the bread.

God will not split open the heavens and give any of us a sign that Jesus' promises are true. Jesus' life stands for itself. Either we believe him or we don't. He, himself, is the only sign we will ever get. Jesus is saying, "You have my word; that's all you need."

Taking up Christ's yoke is another way of describing serious Christian discipleship. A vast chasm separates the hesitant, marginal Christian and the completely dedicated disciple who willingly takes up Christ's yoke.

The reluctant Christian experiences little that is vital and rewarding; the dedicated Christian partakes of the "fulness of the blessing of Christ" (Romans 15:29). One man walks timidly; the other walks confidently. One man lacks God's peace; the other has it.

A mature Christian lawyer in Indiana said, "I've discovered that if I want all of Christ, Christ must have all of me. And as I give myself completely to Christ, he gives himself completely to me."

Obedience to Christ is very closely connected to believing in him. For example, Paul, in referring to Abraham, says that he "believed" God (Romans 4:3). The account in Genesis reports that Abraham ". . . believed the LORD . . ." (Genesis

15:6). But in the words attributed to God himself, we read that ". . . Abraham obeyed my voice . . ." (Genesis 26:5). One account says Abraham *believed;* the other account says Abraham *obeyed.*

A contradiction? Not at all.

The Bible takes it for granted that true belief results in obedience. Faith issues in works. "He who believes in the Son has eternal life; he who does not obey the Son shall not see life, but the wrath of God rests on him" (John 3:36). Belief and obedience compose the two sides of the coin called discipleship.

The Christian disciple obeys, not out of fear, but out of love. Christian obedience unfolds out of a loving and grateful response to Jesus Christ. Discipleship does not stem from an obedience forced out of dread or coercion; it grows out of a freely given response to Christ. A legal relationship is a burden; a love relationship is a blessing.

Recently, I was speaking on a college campus during "religious emphasis week." A brilliant psychology student said to me, "I thought Christians were free—free from the demands of the law. I thought Christians weren't bound by rules and regulations."

What I heard him saying was, "Why do I have to obey Christ anyway? Doesn't freedom mean I'm no longer responsible to the law?"

"Christian freedom doesn't mean the freedom to do as you please," I said. "It means the freedom to allow Christ to help you become your best self."

"Is that what Christian freedom means?" he asked.

"Sure," I replied. "Christian freedom means we are freed from ourselves and our hang-ups so that for the first time in our lives we are free to do what is best for us and best for others. Christian freedom is the liberty to choose Christ's way. Our highest good is to obey God willingly, and to take Christ's yoke upon us. That's true liberty and freedom."

"That makes sense," he responded.

We had a chat together in the college grill about a deeper surrender to Christ's will, and then prayed together. He thanked God for giving him the privilege of taking up Christ's yoke. He later told me that he came into a deeper level of Christian commitment than ever before in his life.

Christ promises the power of the Holy Spirit only to Christians fully committed to his lordship. Luke, the writer of the Acts, speaks of ". . . the Holy Spirit whom God has given to those who obey him" (Acts 5:32).

Taking Christ's yoke means determining to be completely obedient to him in all things. Christ's yoke is not mystical nor something spiritual, but very practical and down-to-earth. When Christians determine to enter into a life of total obedience to Christ, they are taking his yoke upon them. When this happens, life takes on a new dimension.

People often ask, "What does it mean to be a dedicated Christian?" This question is another way of saying, "What is involved in taking Christ's yoke upon yourself?"

Two answers in particular seem to sum up the biblical perspective. Dedicated Christians (1) love God with all their hearts and (2) love their neighbors as themselves. Loving God is the vertical dimension of discipleship; loving one's neighbor is the horizontal dimension. Each presupposes the other. One cannot love God without becoming concerned about his neighbor. On the other hand, one can never develop a true concern for his neighbor unless he loves God.

To be sure, some social activists manifest a concern for others without any reference to God. But concern for one's neighbor in the truest and best sense is impossible unless God's love provides the motivation. We are simply unable to love others in a deep way until God's love fires our hearts with a divine-given compassion.

Soon after I was converted to Jesus Christ, I read in the Bible about the importance of loving God and neighbor. I wondered what it meant to love God with all one's being. Perhaps no one of us has found the full answer to this question, but it certainly must include a regular fellowship with Christ.

I found that the quality of my regular communion with Christ through the day became more vital as I held my daily quiet time. I also found that if I regularly neglected my time of daily prayer, I did not have as close a fellowship with Christ. I came to the conclusion that keeping close to Christ through prayer forms the basis of a life of serious discipleship.

For years, I fluctuated in my daily time of prayer. Sometimes I prayed regularly and at other times I would drift for weeks and weeks, "too busy" to take the time to pray seriously. I gradually came to the conviction that I must stabilize my prayer life if I were really serious in the matter of being a Christian.

Then one day my resolve was strengthened when I heard an Episcopalian priest say, "You must hold your daily quiet time until your quiet time begins to hold you." I determined to begin a life of regular prayer.

I continued my daily prayers for about three months, and then I began to neglect prayer because of the pressure of daily work. I was angry with myself for my lack of discipline and my lack of consistency. I sometimes held my devotions, but as yet they were not holding me. I could not honestly say, "I'd rather pray than do anything else." The glowing reports given by other Christians of a satisfying prayer life only made me more miserable.

Once again, I determined to do something about my irregular prayer life. So I asked God to help me set a time and a place where I could meet with him in daily prayer. I settled on a time and a place and once more began to pray regularly.

Yet, I found that my mind would wander as I prayed. I lapsed into discouragement. Then, quite by accident, I discovered a method of praying that has been a great help to me. I found that if I wrote out a daily prayer, I could exercise better control over my mind. I also discovered that writing forced me to be precise and definite in my praying. I also spend some time in quiet "listening" to God, often writing down my thoughts.

I do not suggest that everyone should write out his prayers. But the practice of doing so has helped me enormously. For this manner of praying has resulted in a needed stability in my prayer life. I have suggested to students and Christians in various places that they add written prayers to their spoken prayers, and many of them report that the technique has greatly helped them in their praying.

Whether you write out your prayers is not of primary importance; but a daily relationship with Christ in prayer *is* primary. Without a sustained and regular fellowship with Christ, we force ourselves to live off our own memories and the secondhand reports of other people's religious experiences. Naturally, such a spiritual diet cannot possibly be as nourishing as a personal and daily encounter with Christ.

Talking with God in prayer and allowing him to talk with us through the Bible and through meditation are simply indispensable to taking up Christ's yoke and becoming a serious disciple.

But discipleship consists of more than praying; discipleship also consists of *doing*. Christ's yoke involves relating to other persons. Contemporary Christian disciples must hear the cry and feel the pain of their neighbors. And hearing and feeling must result in concrete action in their behalf.

The story of the good Samaritan remains one of the best sources for discovering how Christians should relate to others (Luke 10:25-37). Several principles emerge from this story. Our relationshps with others must be (1) flexible, (2) practical, and (3) sacrificial. The good Samaritan adjusted to a new situation; he translated precepts into deeds; and he expended himself for others.

The story of the good Samaritan illustrates the type of outgoing religion of which Jesus approves. The Samaritan was *flexible*. In a moment of stress, he adjusted his personal schedule in order to help the wounded man by the road.

Two religious leaders—a priest and a Levite (a sort of lay associate)—had already passed by the victim who lay sprawled beside the road. Doubtless, the good Samaritan struggled with the temptation to pass by on the other side as the others had done. But he was flexible enough to change his plans and be willing to be interrupted.

I have a personal friend who exemplifies this kind of religion. His name is Russ, and he pastors in a midwestern state. Russ told me of an experience he had once when his wife was away for a week and he was eating his meals in a local restaurant.

One morning, as Russ walked into the restaurant for breakfast, he noticed that only two tables were occupied. At one table sat three well-dressed men—all members of his church. At the other table sat an unshaven and poorly-dressed man whom Russ had never seen before that moment.

Russ's friends spotted him and almost in chorus they said, " 'Morning, pastor."

One of the men, a leading layman, said, "Come on over to our table and we'll buy your breakfast."

Another added, "Yeah, sit down with us and we can chat."

Russ took a second glance at the unknown man at the other table who appeared to be dejected. Then he made a quick decision.

"No, thanks," Russ answered. "I think I'll go over here and eat with this man."

Russ went over and sat down with the stranger, offering him his best smile. Then he said, "Good morning; my name's Russ. What's yours?"

The stranger looked at Russ in almost total unbelief. He started to say something and then decided not to. Instead, he began almost imperceptibly to cry.

"What's the matter?" asked Russ. "Did I say something wrong?"

'No, you didn't say anything wrong," answered the stranger. "It's just that you're the first man that's asked me my name in over nineteen years. You came over here to eat with me instead of your friends. No one has showed me that kind of respect for a long, long time."

Russ related to me, "I just loved him and treated him as I thought Christ would. After our meal, I asked him to eat breakfast with me the next day."

The sequel is that the man started attending Russ's church, and in less than six months he became a vital Christian. Russ reports, "Today, he is a completely changed person. He found a new job and he is alive with the joy of Christ."

My friend Russ can see beyond himself and he is flexible enough to adjust his own plans in order to minister to the needs of others. Surely this kind of religion pleases God.

The Christian disciple who truly emulates his Master looks upon others without respect to class, race, or cultural background. Christ befriended both Jew and Gentile, rich and poor, religious and nonreligious. Like their Lord, Christ's contemporary followers see others as having dignity and worth, regardless of whether they agree at all points.

Outgoing religion is also *practical.* A verbal witness serves best for certain times, while other times call for the practical involvement of deeds. In the story of the good Samaritan, the priest and the Levite probably both made a mental note of the man who had been beaten and robbed.

Perhaps the priest prepared a sermon on the evils of the day. He may have said in his sermon: "Why, only recently I saw the victim of another mugging out on the Jericho road. Yes sir, times are getting worse and worse." Obviously, such a sermon would give little comfort to the man who had been beaten and robbed.

But the Samaritan was practical. He did not take down the man's name and promise to send a camel back for him. Nor did he scold him for traveling alone. Neither did he offer him a Bible to read. Rather, he got down on his knees and became practically involved in his need.

It is difficult today for us to imagine the enormous cultural and religious gap between Jews and the Samaritans. As an illustration, John reports a conversation between Jesus and a Samaritan woman. The woman declared in amazement, "How is it that you, a Jew, ask a drink of me, a woman of Samaria?" John explains: "For Jews have no dealings with Samaritans" (John 4:9).

The priest and the Levite in the story of the good Samaritan certainly would never have beaten and robbed the unfortunate victim lying in the road. The very notion of such an accusation would have shocked them. Yet, they were so preoccupied with their own interests that they offered no practical help. They were not *bad* men, but neither were they *good* men.

Christian discipleship consists of more than passively refraining from hurting others. It actively helps others in ways that are tangible and meaningful. At that point in his life the victim beside the Jericho road needed practical help more than he needed a sermon or a lecture. Christian discipleship demands meaningful service to others as well as sharing with them the good news of the gospel. A well-balanced Christian witness includes deed as well as word.

Outgoing religion is also *expensive.* It costs something to serve Christ. The good Samaritan readily expended his oil and his wine on the injured stranger. He gave up his own beast and he walked. Possibly, the wounded man got blood on the Samaritan's saddle. The Samaritan sacrificed his immediate personal plans; he endangered his reputation by befriending a Jew. He even took the victim to an inn and promised to pay all bills necessary for his recovery.

To some, the actions of the good Samaritan were extravagant. But true discipleship is always costly. Taking up Christ's yoke involves a willingness to avoid the easy way. The committed Christian gladly offers his resources to God, even to the point of sacrifice.

Something of this spirit was displayed by King David. A friend offered to give him the materials for a sacrifice to God. But David refused the offer saying, "No, but I will buy it of you for a price; I will not offer burnt offerings to the LORD my God which cost me nothing" (2 Samuel 24:24). David's devotion to God would not allow him to sidestep personal sacrifice.

Although Christian disciples realize that in giving they receive, they serve others primarily out of loving obedience to Christ. As a result of spending themselves for others they find themselves.

Paul revealed a spiritual law which undergirds this point. "Don't be under any illusion: you cannot make a fool of God! A man's harvest in life will depend entirely on what he sows" (Galatians 6:7 PHILLIPS). Paul is saying, "You get out of life exactly what you put into it."

Jesus gave us a different slant on the same idea: " '. . . Truly, I say to you, as you did it to one of the least of these my brethren, you did it to me' " (Matthew 25:40). He is saying, "The way you treat others is the way you treat me."

Since becoming a Christian, I have been especially conscious of other people. I like people, and I enjoy observing them talk, act, react, and live. As a spectator, I have learned an important lesson: Those who give themselves in service to others are the happiest people I know. It is an unbreakable law: Those who give, find; and those who save, lose.

Jesus addressed his invitation to take up his yoke to all who labor and are heavy laden—that is, to those who find life's burdens heavy. Some of the most common burdens of life are:

> —*guilt,* the burden of the past
> —*boredom,* the burden of the present
> —*fear,* the burden of the future.

Some people carry all of these burdens at once! Little wonder many people find life almost more than they can bear.

Not only do people shoulder the burdens of guilt, boredom, and fear, but they even carry the additional burden of *religion!* Religion becomes a burden when viewed as something one must embrace out of a sense of duty. Such a concept of religion brings one into bondage rather than lifting one out of bondage. The invitation of Jesus is to a life of emancipation, not to the tyranny of legalistic "oughts."

Certainly, the Pharisees and religious lawyers regarded religion as binding rather than as freeing. But Jesus stoutly condemned that sort of religion. He declared, "Woe to you lawyers also! for you load men with burdens hard to bear, and you yourselves do not touch the burdens with one of your fingers" (Luke 11:46). Religous burdens are bad news; the gospel is good news.

A vast difference exists between the burden of religion and the yoke of Jesus. One proves intolerable; the other brings rest to the soul. Jesus' promises remain in effect yet today. "Come to me . . . and I will give you rest. . . . Take my yoke . . . and you will find rest for your souls."

Taking up Christ's yoke means taking seriously Jesus' words "Come to me . . . Follow me . . . Love me . . . Obey me." Christian discipleship does not consist in following *rules* given by Christ. Nor is it content with believing *correct doctrines* about Christ. Discipleship involves a total commitment of one's self to the *person* of Christ.

Discipleship remains man's highest privilege and his greatest opportunity. Those who are truly wise take up Christ's yoke and in so doing find his promised rest.

9

Co-creating With God

WHEN A PERSON becomes Christ's disciple, he not only experiences divine pardon but he is called into a totally new life. Christian conversion means that one's entire orientation moves toward Jesus Christ as iron filings are attracted to a magnet. "When anyone is united to Christ, there is a new world; the old order has gone, and a new order has already begun" (2 Corinthians 5:17 NEB). Christ calls his followers to a life of dynamic creativity. The Christian's destiny is to become a co-creator with God.

As one is converted to Jesus Christ and experiences the new birth, God does something *in* him as well as *for* him. Christian conversion includes receiving the new life of God in one's heart. God imparts the Holy Spirit, and one becomes an entirely new person.

Ezekiel, an Old Testament prophet who spoke for God, told of the time when God would give such life to human beings: "A new heart I will give you, and a new spirit I will put within you; and I will take out of your flesh the heart of stone and give you a heart of flesh" (Ezekiel 36:26).

Peter emphasized that the long-awaited day had arrived: [God's] divine power has granted to us all things that pertain

to life and godliness, through the knowledge of [Christ] . . ."
and we have "become partakers of the divine nature" (2
Peter 1:3,4). Man's highest destiny is to become a partaker of
God's Spirit!

As the Christian remains pliable in God's hands and opens
himself to the Holy Spirit's working, there is no limit set on
what God can do through his life. Great possibilities stretch
out before him.

Modern man's bold optimism regarding his own potential,
while distorted, is in a way well-founded. Man *does* have
almost limitless potential; he *is* capable of greatness.

However, contemporary persons are often deluded at a
crucial point. Many consider man only in terms of what he
can do *by himself,* quite apart from God The error lies not
in believing that man is destined for greatness, but in assuming that man can reach it apart from divine enabling. Whenever our view of man becomes shrouded in a cloak of pride
and self-sufficiency, we develop a pitifully distorted view of
ourselves.

Man's uniqueness consists in his capacity for God. Only
under Christ's lordship can man's possibilities be unleashed
in creative and redemptive ways. Apart from Christ, he
tends to distort his talents and misuse his privileges.

Man may produce great machines, but without God he
uses them for destructive purposes. He may develop the art
of printing to a high degree, but he often uses it to propagate
falsehood and immorality. He may learn how to increase his
years on the earth, but what is the value of an augmented
lifespan if man enjoys little inner peace and spiritual stability?

God created the first man in his own image; then he told

Adam: ". . . fill the earth and subdue it; and have dominion over . . . every living thing . . ." (Genesis 1:28). Such a command reflects God's will that man become a creative person. But in tracing the subsequent history of man, the Bible unfolds the story of how man seriously defaced the image of God within him through his disobedience to God. In doing so, man has failed to achieve the creativity for which he was destined.

Ancient man's mistake consisted in failing to realize that his freedom was freedom *under* God. He wanted, instead, freedom *from* God. Modern man continues to make the same mistake of wanting absolute autonomy and freedom from every restraint, including God.

Some writers who have attempted to correct the arrogant pride of man have, in the process, moved to an extreme position; they picture man as a wretch, a worm, a lump of sin, or as totally and absolutely corrupt. Some contemporary existentialists even insist that man can never rise above the level of a beast. Such over-corrections are strong medicine, little better than the disease. The insistence that man is incapable of any good thing does not harmonize with the teaching of the Bible or our common experience. Man is more than "a worm"; he is created in the image of God. He possesses dignity and infinite worth.

Granted: man is incapable of reaching God through his own unaided powers and he usually gives a lamentably poor account of the stewardship of his talent. But it is not true that man is incapable of rising above the animal level. With God's help, man can reach great heights and perform astounding exploits.

God calls man to creativity—to co-creation with him. However, few persons—including Christians—achieve their maximum creative potential. Since Christians are new persons in Christ, why do they often fail to become creative persons? Several reasons seem to lurk behind this failure.

First, Christians often fail to become as creative as they might because they lack a profound awareness of God. Not that they do not know God, but they fail to experience him on a deep level. Many Christians simply do not enjoy an abiding sense of his presence. The lack of a deep awareness of God obstructs their faith and spiritual vision.

An active faith and a dynamic spiritual vision result only from the unhindered working of the Holy Spirit. Through the active presence of the Holy Spirit in his life, the Christian grows in his awareness of the resurrected Christ. The early Christians in the Book of Acts had a vital experience of the Holy Spirit, and this experience gave them a dynamic which issued in creative living.

Immediately after the early disciples experienced the filling with the Holy Spirit, Peter explained to a large crowd of hearers what had happened: ". . . this is what was spoken by the prophet Joel: 'And in the last days it shall be, God declares, that I will pour out my Spirit on all flesh, and your sons and your daughters shall prophesy, and your young men shall see visions, and your old men shall dream dreams . . .' " (Acts 2:16,17).

Dreaming dreams and seeing visions result from the active indwelling of the Holy Spirit, and they are necessary for creativity. Edison had to see "visions" before he could create his inventions. The founders of the United States had to "dream dreams" before a new nation came to life. Martin

Luther, too, was gripped by something larger than himself before he accomplished his significant and lasting work. Joshua, John the Baptist, Paul, Augustine, St. Francis, John Calvin, John Wesley, E. Stanley Jones, and many others have dreamed dreams; and they have all been creative people. The Holy Spirit gives dreams to men and then translates them into reality.

Perhaps one of our greatest needs today is Christian disciples who are filled with God's Spirit and who see visions and dream dreams with respect to poverty, dehumanizing forces in society, the polluted environment, racial injustices, and the spiritual bankruptcy of our generation.

Conscious disobedience to God at any point grieves the Holy Spirit, strangles creativity, and blocks God's working in our lives. God is never reluctant to work in us, but disobedience indicates *our* reluctance to allow him fully to do so. God cannot work through us unless he has control over us, and our failure to obey him limits his activity in our lives.

Frequently, Jesus pointed out the importance of total obedience to God. For example, he stated, "Blessed . . . are those who hear the word of God and keep it!" (Luke 11:28). On several occasions, Jesus connected man's obedience with God's blessing. He said, "If a man loves me, he will keep my word, and my Father will love him, and we will come to him and make our home with him. He who does not love me does not keep my words . . ." (John 14:23,24). God gives his Spirit to those who keep his word.

However, the Holy Spirit is not a *thing* nor an *influence*; he is a *person*. The Holy Spirit can be lied to (Acts 5:3), grieved (Ephesians 4:30), quenched (1Thessalonians 5:19), and resisted (Acts 7:51). Disobedience to God chokes off the effective ministry of his Spirit in one's life, and a diminished awareness of Christ results. On the other hand, obedience to Christ generates an increased awareness of his presence. And the awareness of Christ opens one to the creative flow of the Holy Spirit.

A second reason Christians fail to become as creative as they might is because of theological confusion. If one does not think correctly he is not likely to act correctly or creatively.

Two common points of confusion cloud the thinking of many sincere Christians. Some Christians try to do everything by themselves because they overstress *law*. Other Christians fail to accomplish much because they misunderstand the nature of *grace*. The first group emphasizes human responsibility; the second group stresses God's activity. But overstress on either—man's responsibility or God's working —leads to imbalance and failure.

Christians who overemphasize duty act as though everything in the Christian life depends on themselves. They seem to think the Christian life revolves around how hard they toil for God. They do not properly grasp the New Testament teaching that the Christian life consists of *God working through man*. Thus, they fail to become creative because they work themselves into a frenzy of activity. Almost constantly, they are nagged by an uneasy conscience which continues to demand more and more activity. They find it hard to relax. The harder they work the more frustrated they become.

I know a housewife who takes it upon herself to shoulder the world's problems. Once her husband gently said to her:

"Sue, God is still able to control the universe; don't worry so much. After all, you can't do *everything* by yourself."

She replied, "If I don't worry, who else will?"

It is easy to fall into the trap of thinking that the whole of the Christian life depends on us. I know of one businessman who began to make real headway against his habit of nervous overactivity. He typed out the following verse and read it daily as he shaved: ". . . for God is at work in you, both to will and to work for his good pleasure" (Philippians 2:13). He discovered that the secret of creative living is *God working in man.*

God at work in man: The creative Christian never forgets it. Christ's disciples are not called to frenetic labor, as if everything depended on their own striving. One of Christ's last promises remains especially important: ". . . remember, I am with you always, even to the end of the world" (Matthew 28:20 PHILLIPS). Because Christ promises to be with us, we do not have to walk alone.

But there are other Christians who fall into a different sort of error. They stress that God's activity is everything, and they think that *nothing* depends on what they do; they minimize human responsibility. These Christians tend to misuse their Christian freedom and presume on God's grace.

One well-meaning Christian poultry farmer named Sam said to me, "My salvation hinges completely on God's grace; don't you agree?"

"Sure, but man has a part to play also," I answered.

"What do you mean?" said my friend. "Don't you believe in God's grace?"

"Of course I do," I replied. "I believe that the entire Christian life, from start to finish, rests on the grace of God. But our salvation *hinges* on our *response* to God's grace."

"I don't know . . . ," said Sam.

I said, "Sam, I completely agree that we can't lift a finger to save ourselves; our redemption is totally a work of God's grace. But since we aren't robots we still have the ability to say no to God's offer of grace."

"I suppose so," muttered Sam.

"That's why I prefer to say that our salvation hinges on our *response* to God's grace," I concluded.

But Sam did not accept what I said. Later, he told a mutual friend that since God loved him he would no longer be held accountable for any sin he might choose to commit. Sam's attitude was, "Nothing depends on me; everything rests on God. What I do doesn't matter—I'm going to let God do it all."

Sam's attitude was contrary to Paul's advice, ". . . present your bodies as a living sacrifice, holy and acceptable to God . . ." (Romans 12:1). Persons who do not surrender themselves to God for his daily using cannot expect to become creative. Christians who fail to see the importance of offering themselves to God greatly hinder God's working in them.

Thus, some Christians fail to become creative because they expect God to do everything for them—even make their decisions for them. And others fail to become creative because they try to do everything themselves. A true view of creative discipleship lies in the middle, between these two extreme positions.

All the power for the Christian life comes from God, but God expects us to yield ourselves to him for his using. ". . . yield yourselves to God as men who have been brought from death to life, and your members to God as instruments of righteousness" (Romans 6:13). When Christians yield themselves to God and their physical bodies to his service, they can become co-creators with God.

A third reason Christians fail to become as creative as they might stems from lack of faith. Faith remains a mystery to many Christians but it need not. Faith is simply believing God's promises and receiving them into one's life.

Christian faith is not an attitude which one can exercise in a vacuum; faith is relational—that is, it must be placed in someone. For instance, I know a young housewife who found it difficult to cope with the stresses in her daily life. She had four young children (two of whom were in diapers), and she was constantly worried about finances.

A neighbor tried to encourage her by saying, "Marilyn, have faith! Just have faith!"

Marilyn took a long and serious look at her would-be comforter and said, "Have faith in what?" Not until she turned to Jesus Christ did faith have any meaning.

Marilyn was on to something important. She knew that she could not just have faith. There must be an *object* for her faith, someone in whom she could place her confidence and trust. For the Christian, that Someone is Jesus Christ; he is the object of faith. ". . . all the promises of God find their Yes in him" (2 Corinthians 1:20).

Saying prayers cannot be equated with exercising faith. Asking God repeatedly for help for the same thing may indicate a *lack* of faith. Faith accepts and appropriates what God offers.

A friend of mine, named Aaron, told me how he learned

to exercise greater faith in God. Aaron reported, "I used to find myself going through the day asking God, 'Help me, Lord; help me, Lord.' " Aaron continued, "One day it occurred to me that my constant cry, 'Help me, Lord; help me, Lord' was more of a whine than a prayer. I wasn't really believing that God was helping me at all."

"I see what you mean," I said.

Aaron went on to say, "I realized that a much better prayer would be to ask God to help me at the beginning of the day, and then throughout the day acknowledge his help by saying, 'Thank you that you *are* helping me, Lord.' " Aaron went on to say, "Now I really believe he *is* helping me. And I *receive* his help instead of just whimpering for him to help me. That's what true faith is."

Ever since my conversation with Aaron, I've tried what he suggested. And it really works. God wants Christians to believe him and to receive from him. Without believing and receiving, our prayers display little faith. And remember: Faith brings God's creativity into our lives.

Most Christians could do far more than they presently do if they believed more firmly in God. They would become more creative if they learned to accept God's gift of creativity. God could do more exciting and creative things in all our lives if we confidently expected him to work. Faith is asking and receiving from God.

The biblical promises regarding God's creative activity in the life of the Christian are all connected with faith. Consider the following verses:

— " 'According to your faith be it done to you' "
(Matthew 9:29).

— ". . . whatever you ask in prayer, you will receive, if
you have faith" (Matthew 21:22).
— "The victory that defeats the world is our faith . . ."
(1 John 5:4 NEB).
— ". . . without faith it is impossible to please him"
(Hebrews 11:6).

Embedded in the last words of Jesus to his disciples is this
statement: ". . . I have prayed for you that your faith may not
fail . . ." (Luke 22:32). And in Jesus' teaching about the last
days he asks, "Nevertheless, when the Son of man comes, will
he find faith on earth?" (Luke 18:8). Clearly, Jesus is saying
that he will respond to the faith of those who exercise it.

Some of Jesus' most positive statements were made with
reference to people's faith; some of his most negative statements lamented their lack of faith. Faith brings God's
creativity into the life of the Christian, and faith makes it
possible for him to reach his highest potential.

Thus, creativity depends on these three things:

—becoming more aware of God
—acting in harmony with God's principles
—receiving by faith God's working in one's life.

These are the requisites for creativity. But just what does it
mean to be creative?

In the first place, to be creative is to express one's self in an
individual and highly personal way. Creative Christian discipleship cannot be contained in a predetermined pattern of
living any more than a unique sculpture can be mass-pro-

duced on a drill press. No detailed model for creative living can be universally applied; God has a custom-tailored plan for each life. God's plan for every Christian involves the development of his own uniqueness.

Christian discipleship is sometimes blamed for turning people into dull conformers to a lifeless tradition. *Religion* may produce a dull sameness in people, but Christianity does not. Sameness and conformity are non-Christian attitudes which have intruded into our thinking. God created our human personalities with an even greater variety than autumn leaves, snowflakes, or sunsets. God does not desire that any Christian become a carbon copy of another. Even those of us who are one-talent people have possibilities that cannot be duplicated by five-talent persons.

The church is at its best when it encourages every Christian to be his own individual self and to express his uniqueness in creative ways. Every Christian—regardless of his occupation—is called to creative living.

Creativity is not restricted to such activities as composing symphonies, writing sonnets, and painting portraits. Such accomplishments are of course creative, but creativity includes much more. Only a few people have the talents for work such as composing, writing, and painting. If creativity were limited to these activities, most of us could never become creative people. But God wills that every person express his own unique creativity in such daily activities as rearing a family, teaching a class, running a business or driving a truck.

Each person has received from God the talents and gifts necessary for a creative life. Paul assured the Christians of his time, ". . . grace was given to each of us according to the measure of Christ's gift. Therefore it is said, '. . . he gave gifts to men' " (Ephesians 4:7,8). God's gifts are given to *all* Christians; any Christian can be a creative person.

In the story of creation, Genesis gives the following account: "The earth was without form and void, and darkness was upon the face of the deep; and the Spirit of God was moving over the face of the waters. And God said, 'Let there be light'; and there was light" (Genesis 1:2,3). God created order out of chaos; he made beauty out of ugliness; he changed darkness into light.

Creation is making something good out of something which is not yet good, and God calls his disciples to this type of activity in the world today. To turn an enemy into a friend is to be creative; to encounter a difficult day with faith and optimism is to be creative; to return good for evil is to be creative.

When a housewife meets the confusion of a busy household and brings loving order to it, she is creative. When a teacher meets an apathetic class and makes learning an adventure, she is creative. When a businessman sincerely serves the best interests of others, he is creative. When a truck driver meets an impossible situation with courage and integrity, he is creative. Creativity is bringing your unique contribution to a potentially bad situation or to a situation which is not yet good.

To be a creative Christian also means to be Christlike. God is supremely concerned about the development of our moral character. Our era tends to emphasize *doing*, to the neglect of *being*. God begins with what we are because our being conditions all our acting.

Even though the Christians of the Middle Ages were not

without moral blemishes, they were right in stressing the importance of one's religious life. These people remain a continual reminder to us today. Their point of view harmonized with the New Testament. Paul writes that God has "ordained that [we] should be shaped to the likeness of his Son . . ." (Romans 8:29 NEB). Creativity includes having one's life reshaped in the image of Christ himself.

At many points, Christlike virtues run counter to the values of our current generation. We are taught to dominate; Christ calls us to serve. We want to acquire; Christ calls us to give. We tend to gauge experiences with reference to self; Christ urges us to measure experiences with reference to God. Many of our personal difficulties and national problems stem from our tendency to substitute our own value system for that of Christ.

For the Christian, the measure by which all else can be judged is Jesus Christ. Christ does more than point to truth; he *is* truth. He does more than tell us how to live; he provides the inner power for living. He is not merely an advisor for the Christian life, nor just an example to the Christian; he *is* the Christian life.

Creativity in the Christian sense transcends the discovering of ways to make life more pleasant physically. Christian creativity goes beyond the inventing of machines to make life more convenient. True creativity relates primarily to the full development of our humanity, and it touches us at the deepest levels of our existence. Christian creativity involves living in Christ's way and in Christ's power. Creativity expresses itself most significantly in relating to life's joys, sorrows, frustrations, and opportunities in a Christlike manner.

And finally, Christian creativity must be expressed in a

servant posture. Christ works through his disciples in order that they can minister to others. Christian creativity cannot be expressed in a solitary vacuum; it must be directed toward the good of others. Christian creativity must be related to the arena of daily life and to the world of human beings around us.

Often, the actual deed of the Christian is not as significant as the spirit in which the deed is performed. Maintaining a Christlike attitude in the face of adversity can become a creative act. A cup of cold water given in the spirit of Christ can become a creative deed of healing and reconciliation. When one lives his daily life in the context of sincere commitment to Christ, Christ takes his most feeble efforts and multiplies them many times over to the blessing of others. Christian living of this sort demands a radical surrender to Christ, for without his indwelling we are powerless to live in a Christlike fashion.

Several months after my conversion to Jesus Christ, I faced a crisis in my Christian life. It was a crisis of Christ's lordship. I knew Christ as the One who had forgiven me and imparted to me a new spiritual life. But I was beginning to see that I was going to have to go deeper with Christ or else back up from my commitment. For several weeks I tried desperately to serve Christ and at the same time have my own way. I was not succeeding, and I knew it.

One evening, before going to bed, I laid out my frustration before Christ in prayer. I prayed, "I want to be a Christian, but these past days have been the most miserable in my life. I want to serve you, but sometimes my own desires threaten to cancel my commitment to you as Lord."

I sensed Christ's attitude toward me. It was an attitude of

unbelievable love. Even when I had taken my own way instead of Christ's way, he continued to love me. I seemed to hear Christ saying to me, "I can bless you and make you into your highest self only if you let me have complete control."

I wanted to surrender more fully to Christ, but I was afraid to trust him because I didn't want to be disappointed. Finally, after a prolonged struggle, I turned over my present and my future to Christ. And my consecration included even my hesitancy and my fears. After a simple prayer, God came to me in a new way, and my life has never been the same!

God did not receive my consecration because I was worthy, but because I was willing. That is all he asks of any of us. Anyone can begin to live a life of complete dependence on Christ which will lift him into a new level of human existence. God can become more real to you than you ever dared to believe!

Creative living results in personal fulfillment. Frequently, Christ uses such words as *happy, joy, rejoice,* and *peace.* The most concentrated discussion of happiness in all literature is found in the section of Jesus' teachings to his disciples, called the Beatitudes. The word *blessed* (which literally means *happy*) appears in almost every verse. Christ taught much about it, but happiness eludes millions of persons.

The good news of the Christian gospel is that happiness and fulfillment can begin now! The happiness which Christ offers to all men unfolds not as a promise of future bliss or of "pie in the sky by and by." Rather, it shines as a present possibility which we can experience in the present.

For many people, happiness depends on circumstances or possessions. Or, sometimes contemporary writers depict happiness as a matter of chance or an accident that lies completely beyond man's control. Such views of happiness savor of pre-Christian paganism which desperately bargained with the gods so that they might choose to smile on man.

But Christian happiness is not dependent upon chance or the capricious whims of fate. Christ freely offers happiness to each disciple; joy is the birthright of all God's children. Jesus promised, ". . . no one will take your joy from you" (John 16:22). The way of Christ is the way of happiness. And the happiness which is rooted in Christ permeates the creative life of his disciples.

An ancient prophet declared, ". . . the eyes of the LORD run to and fro throughout the whole earth, to show his might in behalf of those whose heart is blameless toward him" (2 Chronicles 16:9). You can be such a person—you can become a Christian disciple in deed and in truth. Then you can begin to co-create with God, and you will experience as thousands of others the joys of Christian discipleship.